Kellogg Harrison Family & Relationship Series
Communication & Conflict Resolution

Pathways To Intimacy

Communicating With Care & Resolving Differences

by: Marvel Elizabeth Harrison, Ph.D.
and Terry Kellogg, M.A.

BRAT Publishing ❖ 369 Montezuma, Ste 203 ❖ Santa Fe, NM 87501
1-800-359-2728

Cover art from *Reflections* by Greg Michaels

Harrison, Marvel • Kellogg, Terry • Michaels, Greg
ISBN 1-880257-08-4

BRAT Publishing, 369 Montezuma, Suite 203, Santa Fe, NM 87501 1-800-359-2728 FAX 1-505-662-4044
Printed in USA

Pathways To Intimacy is dedicated
to all families who maintain love by
going beyond the differences

We would like to especialy thank Linda Pruitt of
the Mulberry Center who has continued to
believe in us and our work and who created
a home for our ***Life Balance***™ **Program**, offering
hope and goodness for many people.

Pathways To Intimacy

PART ONE

THE POWER OF SHARING

Communicating with Care

The Power of Sharing
Communicating With Care

Introduction

"Communication is the foundation of culture, family and friendship. Learn listening as active loving. If we can't talk it out we'll act it out."

Communication is the expression of belonging and relationship in community. The family is the basic building block of community. Communication is the way we share who we are, where we've been and what's happened to us. Communication includes the stories, rituals, tales, songs, dance, and ceremonies of shared traditions carrying on our history.

The importance of communication in developing community is illustrated in the biblical story of the Tower of Babel. The tower was becoming an overpowering focus, so God gave everyone 'new tongues.' The people parted into smaller groups according to their shared new language. When communication breaks down, working together becomes difficult and the group relationships splintered.

Communication is the ability to relate and convey ideas, images, history and emotions. It is the distinguishing feature of the human family. The gifts of speech, writing and art are the sharing with others the realities we perceive and express. In conversation we tend to focus on the words of a shared experience and miss the natural forms of communication of body posture, touch, scent, facial expression and non-verbal sound. Many of us have become physically, sexually, and emotionally quiet, not utilizing the full range of our ability to communicate.

With a focus on written and spoken forms of communication it becomes easier to manipulate, relate dishonestly and build false connection through word alone. Dishonesty and disconnection are major causes of cultural breakdown in society and family.

Open and honest communication is the basis of intimate and loving relationships. It is the healing of discord and can bring about wisdom and innovation. To withdraw and become non-communicative is a punishing posturing while openly expressing what's in our heart can be a loving posture.

The extremes of any posture create problems. The fallacy inherent in complete openness and honesty, "to always tell the truth and talk about everything" causes unrealistic expectations and sets up problems. Honesty isn't everything. In caring relationships we'll do some protecting of partners and children around our ongoing thoughts and fears. Even the program of AA for recovering alcoholics speaks of rigorous, not perfect honesty. Honesty tied with gentleness, care, guardianship and an awareness of passing feelings and thoughts can help cement a relationship. Just as dishonesty can destroy a relationship or be used to hurt others, honesty can also hurt.

Having to "tell all" reflects the absence of privacy and can frighten, punish or set us up for trouble. Time heals, the past is just the past and most issues are fleeting. Telling all is important if the reality is likely to be felt and reacted to. Remember, there are no secrets, only denial and all denial gets acted out.

We cannot communicate, even our withdrawal communicates the anger or fear we feel in our displeasure or depression. To glance away speaks volumes, while holding a glance with joy speaks treasures. Shared silence can be a deepening of communication while isolating silence can be deafening and painful.

Within each of us dwells an artist, a poet, a romantic and an idealist. To share our visions and ideals is the addition of our verse to the expanding hymns of the universe. Joining our voices in song, drawing or writing involves overcoming the fear of inadequacy and the reactions of others. This risk offers us a chance to achieve fulfillment of our limitless possibilities. Within the word communication lies the roots for such words as community, communion, commitment, compassion. Com means with - we are with others, ourselves and our environment. The withness we feel lies in the communication we experience.

Self Communication

Integrity, the integration of various aspects of self, and self with community rests on healthy communication with self. The ongoing conversation we have in our mind is the reflection of our integration and self concept. This mental communication might be a pre-recorded message from earlier times, usually childhood. If our thought talk is negative, critical, anxiety ridden or focuses on perfection it erodes our self confidence and esteem while deeply affecting our ability to take healthy risks and enjoy the journey of our lives.

The voice within need not be quieted but altered to one of a gentle and supportive mental companion reflecting our inner wisdom and integrity. We have to review and process the source of the sabotaging messages, be they from past trauma, losses, or feedback from others before the alteration of the message to a positive affirmation can take place. The transformation from negative to positive self communication is a gradual one. It takes a willingness to look honestly at the past, as well as the courage and perseverance to live within the voiced range of our inner wisdom and the strength to practice healthy affirmations while maintaining a balanced lifestyle. When we lose balance the inner dialogue reflects this imbalance with messages of anger, despair and fear.

Affirmations are a form of healthy self communication. They are gifts we give others and ourselves. They're easier to give when we've received them. Living in healthy, affirming settings where we're noticed is a prerequisite for internalizing the supportive messages to ourselves.

Much of our communication with self and others is simply a reflection and reenactment of how others have communicated with us. To inspire honesty and depth of sharing we need to find communities offering us honesty, depth and safety for us to practice.

Our communication with those closest to us becomes a mirror of our self communication. If we are judgmental, critical, angry and anxious in our self talk we will project the same out to those closest to us. We may be able to be supportive of people outside our immediate family but those closest will feel the edge of our self contempt and impatience.

Culture and Meaning

Expressions of deep communication come in many forms. Practicing crafts and trades give us a chance to communicate with and through our work. Communicating through form, design and function is an expression of art. The designers of automobiles, clothing, furniture, airplanes and landscape all communicate in art and form. We practice communicating in sales, advertising, teaching and in building, be it a mall, a chair, a business or a book.

We are creatures with a calling, our calling is to communicate through our art, the experience of our uniqueness and our connection with creation. In our culture the position, place and prestige of the artist has been lost and in its loss we lose the symbols and myth, the deepest interpretations of meaning and culture. When the place of art as communication is elevated and when each of us learn the expressions of our artistic talent, whether in sciences, mathematics, music, construction, engineering, teaching or whatever, our culture is enriched and enlivened.

Culture dies when we lose the relatedness, the communication between all creatures, all disciplines, all life and all creation. The meaning of oneness is the communicating of inspiration. The recognition of ourselves as on going vehicles of creation and the acceptance of community will inspire us to go to heroic efforts to preserve what is created and honor the process of creation.

Communication is a search for meaning, wisdom, beauty, sense and order. We find these in the rituals, symbols and myths of past storytellers and path makers who left directions for the journey in their stories, art, dreams and lore. In our wisdom we can interpret, integrate and honor the symbols and myths from the various cultures within and outside of our society. We can then discover the themes, philosophy and meaning of life.

History is rich in communication and each piece of creation shares the history and has it's own story for us to watch and learn from. The Dalai Lama said "The birds are my teachers" and so are trees and rivers, owls and grasshoppers. Each communicates a miracle. Each sings a unique song. Each is an artistic particle of the mosaic of creation. The relationship with each can be honored just as the experienced rock climber feels and communicates with the rock face, the mason feels and knows the stone, the parent touches and understands the infant, the mechanic intuits the engine. In deep communication with what is around us we touch the "quality" and offer reverence to the uniqueness and beauty creating a community of connected and committed spirituality.

Communication in Families

Attending means we respond in communication in a manner reflecting the other person's presence, intensity and quality. Many of the following suggestions are part of attending.

Communication is the adhesive force of families. Bonding is reflected and maintained through communicating. In a group with little or no bonding the members in their isolation substitute the communication with manipulation, dishonesty, or seduction. When bonding is overdone the members may be enmeshed and feel stuck, unable to change and grow, the communication of new ideas and spontaneity are stifled. Communication reaches its highest form when there is a sense of community balanced with respect for the individual and both detachment and connection are valued. Bonding is based on healthy boundaries, allows space, flexibility and affirms uniqueness, giving fertile soil for learning, awareness and open sharing.

Even though we cannot *not* communicate, we can and often do communicate without care or awareness of what we are sending or how we are sending it. We may send 'mixed messages' - one message in words, another with our facial expressions, eyes and body language. Our voice tone and inflections may send yet other messages. These mixed messages cause misunderstandings and often offend. When we practice congruence, the words, delivery and posture of the deliverer are matching, so communication can build understanding.

Learning to understand feelings and use the language of feelings gives us the tools to express ourselves to others at a deeper level. When we are immersed in feelings we will be able to continue talking our way through the overwhelm rather than fall further into them. *Feelings we don't talk out we will act out.*

The language of feelings allows us to enjoy emotional fluency - having our internal and feeling experience match our words, body language and external experience, resulting in clear messages of who we are and what we want to share. Healthy emotional sharing requires the appropriate expression and suppression of feelings and the ability to detach some from the feelings to facilitate communication in certain settings. The more emotionally fluent we become, the more the people around us will experience congruence with their own feelings.

Non Verbal Communication

Most of the communication in family is nonverbal. It's not what is said but how and where it's said that communicates. A family member's statement "It's cold in this room." may be a simple noticing of temperature, a request for someone to bring a sweater or blanket or turn up the heat or for a comment on the furnace not having been repaired, a noticing of the mood of those in the room or any number of other possibilities. The words used comprise only a small portion of what is said.

It's important to not over interpret or over ascribe meaning to nonverbal body posture or mood swings. A distancing or non communicative posture can mean something other than malevolence - maybe the person is tired or has a headache. Silence or withdrawal may not express anger, meanness, or disappointment but might come from a need for safety or a time to process.

Controlling Styles

Sometimes people cut off communication with others by talking above the listener, using language the listener can't understand, interrupting, over questioning, diversion, ignoring, interrupting or intimidating body postures.

Some people refuse to accept different speech patterns, choosing to focus on "proper" speech styles and techniques rather than listening to what is being shared. Over correcting speech breaks down the willingness to share. Most speech patterns and styles are a reflection of culture including ethnic heritage, socio/economic level, geographic location and age. The differences present increased richness and wealth of information. The model of the 'Queen's' English may not be a valid concept for people who don't recognize themselves as the Queen's subjects!

A voice can be a tool for control, intimidation or seduction. Some preachers, speakers and parents tend to use the above. The power of a voice has few limitations - consider Adolph Hitler. What does it feel like to be yelled at? Shouting can engender rage or force people back into passivity. At a large conference, a speaker with an evangelical style of presentation ended his talk by taking a very powerful pose close to the audience, his arms in the air, shaking his finger and shouting, "The last thing I want you to remember is that I love each and everyone of you. And, if you can't handle that, then that's your problem!" The message did not come across to everyone as very loving or accepting but rather as over done and attacking.

Another controlling posture lies in the opposite extreme. Speaking very quietly forces everyone to strain to listen. The quiet voice can be seductive, conspiring and manipulative imposing as much as the booming voice. There are appropriate times and places for both extremes of voice projection for sharing messages.

Seductive and over emotional sharing is very controlling. A parent divorced for several years and still speaking to the children in a highly charged and emotional manner about the other parent, places the children in a bind between the berated parent and the complaining parent. The hostility frequently becomes the controlling force of connection within the family. A speaker who sobs at the exact same point of a lecture over and over bonds to each audience through sincerity and vulnerability while actually acting.

Language is often used to demean people who speak differently. Good communicators speak in the language of the listener in a non mimicking fashion. They listen for the richness and art of dialect, noting colloquialisms and nuances as a way of gaining insight.

A strong communicator will join in another's world with use of their language in a respectful way. When traveling, even the attempt to use words of the local language reflects respect and is usually appreciated. Messages can also be shared without words but with our hands, eyes, and facial expressions. Listening with our eyes is an empowering way of communicating. We can speak volumes when we allow grace and love to flow from within to those around us.

Semantics of communicating can be fascinating and observing the development and changes of words and their meanings can guide us into other people's worlds since language is an identifying and unifying force. Adolescents have a vocabulary all their own. Every job, profession or career has its own occupational language of technical terms and lingo shared. Entry into the world of advanced technology requires the mastery of 'high tech' language. Certain endeavors create a communication cult, leaving non users on the outside. To enter a career or new group it's necessary to learn the language.

Word pressure abounds. The incorrect politics of politically correct speech has created tension, putting people on edge and forcing an unwillingness to discuss important topics. The hyper sensitivity of various groups to assumed slams and slanders is creating a culture of articulated innocuousness'. How does one discuss programs or facilities for the handicapped when they don't know what to call the handicapped? An uptight reaction to word mistakes is a reflection of crabby people looking for slights and ignoring the core problems of the culture.

Maybe the real problems are too big and we feel helpless about dealing with them causing us to be hyper sensitive, attempting to construct boundaries with use of politically correct language. Such boundaries are external and external boundaries are rigid, easily violated, even by the most caring of people who mean well. Is it worth driving a good hearted person away over their use of words? On the other hand, there is no excuse not to listen to people, respecting requests for preferred language and hearing needs. Seek what is genuine. Leave the rest, regardless of the semantics.

Special Words and Ways

Words have a felt sense. Consider the power in words - phony, evil, terrorize, rape, criminal, offender, molest, sue, force, militant, and cheat. And the gentleness of soothe, nurture, fuzzy, brook, kindred, tender, breeze. Funny sounding words can make us giggle - kangaroo, kiwi, butter brickle, turbot, locomotive, burp, tantalize, piglet, belly button, chataqua.

There are also words of encouragement and support - pride, sensitivity, caring, noticing, affirming rather than words of competitiveness and discouragement - loser, cheater, lazy, selfish, stubborn.

Making up new words to share can create a special bonding between people. 'Cercee,' pronounced (sir'-see) in our family means a pleasant little surprise, maybe a small gift or treat given when least expected. Besides creating new words, there's the fine art of 'creative spelling' with the words we now use. W.C. Fields once said, "Anyone who can't spell a word more than one way is a real dummy!"

A benign sense of humor in communicating sprinkles interest and surprise and can blend warmth and objectivity. Even serious communication need not be morbid, but morbid communication is always serious. Humor short cuts shame, diffuses pain and bridges distance. Humor is the soaring spirit of our humanness. Maybe the joke is on all of us!

Laughter is the universal language. It knows no dialects though remains unique to the wearer, coming in many shapes and sizes of bursts, chuckles, snorts, hisses and guffaws. Laughter is the communication of our humor. Communication comes easiest when we refuse to take ourselves too seriously, when we can laugh at our selves, our foibles, idiosyncrasies and mistakes.

Regardless of how much we read, study, learn, practice and fine tune our communication skills, we will inevitably miscommunicate with people. The better versed we become, the less likely it is to happen and the sooner we will recognize it when it does. The best communicators are people who are able to own their part in missed communication and are willing to take the risk to reach toward rather than away.

A Note On Censorship - Every Song We Sing

Every song we sing
Once was never heard
It started with a single voice
Singing a heart-felt word

How many songs have been lost
How many voices gone unheard
When child hearts are broken

Our dreams are wishes from the heart
How many dreams have gone undreamt
With child rights unspoken

Visions are blossoms of the mind
Hope is seed for tomorrow
These are the gifts of healing
When a child has been cherished

We do not agree with censorship, certainly good taste, respect and freedom to make choices are a healthier alternative. Ignorance, an educational system designed for a few, poverty - these are the true forms of censorship in our culture. We do not have to burn books if no one is interested or able to read them. We do not have to quiet voices of dissent if no one risks dissenting or is not articulate enough to voice the dissension. Cultural illiteracy and despair flow out of poverty and family as well as community violence.

Thirty-six Suggestions for Listening and Sharing

❖❖❖❖❖

Eye contact Listen with your eyes Listen to their eyes

We speak and listen with our eyes. Healthy comunication, in many cultures begins with and is sustained through eye contact. Holding eye contact is not staring. There will be movement and shifts but the expression in our eyes can reflect care and understanding as well as hearing. The speaker can feel safe and held in the energy of our gaze. How often have people we care about, our partners, our children, shared what's important to them while our eyes are glued to a TV, a book or a newspaper? At social gatherings we may be engaged in conversation while scanning the setting. The message we give when we look away is to stay away. This is true for new people and those already in our life. If we can't give full attention now, we can state a time, preferably in the near future when can. In the decision to set a future time for the conversation, we need to evaluate our priorities carefully. Is our favorite soap opera or the news more important than a child's message to us? Often our children, spouses and partners approach us with enthusiasm, wanting a connection, time, attention, not just wanting to talk. Putting down the newspaper or turning off the TV can show them our priorities.

❖❖❖❖❖

Body posture

Along with eye contact, facing the person we are communicating with directly and openly in a relaxed manner enables them to communicate more freely. Our bodies' reflect our attention. We listen with our bodies and we listen to their bodies. A comfortable body posture reflects a comfortable communication. In maintaining eye contact and body posture it's helpful if the eyes of the listener are on the same level as the eyes of the speaker. In reacting physically to the information we hear, our understanding can be reflected, with a look of chagrin or change of facial expression, reaching out, or a hand gesture. Slightly leaning forward is an indication of increased interest, or a reflection of the intensity of something being shared. Keeping our legs or arms unfolded is a way of letting more in and letting them feel we are with them. Using appropriate body posture involves reacting physically. Active listening techniques include nodding our head, making gestures, and smiling. Sometimes we can react with humor and approval and reflect these in our physical being. We can also reflect physically the feelings of privilege to be communicating with this person. We can encourage them with our expressions, our bodies and with touch to continue to be open. Be gentle and physically non intrusive to provide safety and trust.

❖❖❖❖❖

Offer feed-back React verbally

The verbal reaction indicates connection and understanding. Small verbal gestures like "yes," "I see," "sounds like it," or "oh," can encourage and reflect. Sometimes even just a sound will do. When offering others feedback, being brief and precise, still allows the other person to be in the sharing position. Keep feedback relevant to what's shared and avoid speaking in riddles or mysteries. If we overdo feedback while someone is sharing we may overwhelm and inhibit their ability to continue. Lecturing breaks the connection and the point of the lecture is generally lost. A simple statement of the point can be inserted and received without breaking the safety and mutuality of sharing. In our verbal reactions the inflection can mean as much as the word or more. We can say "oh" and the inflection of "oh" could mean surprise or "oh, so that's how it is" or "oh, that's a little shocking" or "oh, so what." But the "oh" usually creates an opening for them to enter our life with theirs. Feedback in the form of a word or short sentence allows the opening to widen.

❖❖❖❖❖

Avoid judgments and moralizing

Saying what is right or wrong can reduce options and discovery as well as close off future communication. Obviously some things are destructive and/or illegal and we need to maintain our own integrity, rather than be collusive. We can present what we see in a gentle way, by helping to clarify values and options rather than imposing our code. "Judge not lest ye be judged." Judging is usually shaming. On the other hand, we all make judgments. As long as we stay flexible and not project our judgments in a rigid way, our judgments don't have to be a shaming experience. There's a balance between hiding judgments and imposing them. Being open to other's choices and affirming their courage or acknowledging the person is doing their best and will come through it with wisdom helps the sharer seek their own values. When requested, it's OK to share what we believe to be the best course or what we would do or want to do. We can still leave the options open for other courses or actions. We all tend to move through our hardest times better when we are affirmed in our choices and our intent even when we mess up. We don't have to agree with someone to affirm them. We can affirm the feelings, the intent, the courage, the ownership, the openness, and many other aspects of the conversation and their choices. Most of us self judge a great deal, so we seldom need others to judge for us. When we focus too much on what we disagree with, we create defensiveness in the other person, shutting down openness in communication.

❖❖❖❖❖

React emotionally

Feedback feelings in a balanced way without being overly emotional. If we are connected at a feeling level and involved, it creates a safe setting for the communication to be at an emotionally honest level. If we "stay cool," or aloof or don't share our emotional reaction in a way matching what's said, we are giving a message of not caring; a detachment that isn't true. Allowing a tear to fall when we hear something sad, joining in the anger with a statement like "I'm angry that happened to you," or providing a statement of concern or fear, "I feel a sense of fear as you describe it," all help build and encourage further sharing. It's important we don't overwhelm with our emotional reality. Sharing our feelings in a mild and gentle way helps others avoid feeling responsible or guilty for causing us pain and fear. Over-dramatizing our feelings for the sake of connection will produce the opposite effect. Dishonest reactions only teach dishonesty.

Notice, label and affirm feelings

Congruency and fluency are key parts of communicating. Words are just words, but words can reflect inner hurt, pain or joy. If we notice the words and label the feeling, we offer a gift to the other person. In the labeling we can also affirm and let them know their feeling is a natural reaction. "Given what's going on, it is likely one would feel that way." We can connect the feelings to what is happening. Our feelings are healthy responses yet we tend to fight the feeling and enter verbal, physical and emotional turmoil with ourselves. In our communications with others, staying congruent with our own feelings enables us to be more affirming and noticing of theirs. Doing the labeling can be done as suggestion rather than a hard statement. "You seem to be feeling angry," or "I believe that must be a scary situation to be in," or "You sound angry as you speak of this," "I notice the sadness in you eyes," or "From the tone of your voice it sounds like fear." When we're experiencing our feelings, we often do not have the label for the experience. An outside source helping label the feeling gives us the ability to deal with it appropriately. Affirming needs to accompany the label. This can be done with a statement such as "I know I would be feeling angry if I were experiencing what you are," or "I think it's courageous to show the anger about this situation," possibly, "It seems to me, that crying about this is an important part of the healing." If what is shared was a loss, the feelings are generally part of the grieving process and grieving is how we provide closure in the healing of losses so we can move on to the new. It can be helpful to notice the grieving with, "It seems like you lost something, and this feeling is a part of your grieving." Being able to connect the feeling to the loss enables us to move through the grieving process.

❖❖❖❖❖

Joining

Put yourself in their shoes, while keeping a perspective. Imaging ourselves in their position increases understanding. Keeping perspective and joining enables us to feel and expose the binds, the stuck places, options and feelings. When communicating, especially with children, to be "with" them, to join them in the wanting is a way of affirming the desire without being responsible for providing. The desire may be "I want a horse" rather than replying, "You know we live in an apartment building and they don't allow it" the joining response could be, "Wouldn't that be wonderful!

We could ride our horse and do errands, and take it for a gallop, and horses are such beautiful animals!" Even a response to the next question, "Can we get one?" need not be a hard, fast "no." A willingness to check out rules and costs can sometimes be done without raising hopes too much. Even the willingness to go horseback riding together or some other type of compromise about a different kind of pet may be an alternative. Communication is a balance between affirming dreams and supporting realism. In joining, we see the importance and find the path to making dreams come true, or at least opening up options for possible fulfillment or new dreams. Embrace the background of the dream or wish. Rather than saying "no" or "that's impossible," look at the journey and see the request as a shared communication. If a child says "I hate this house" we could reply "Maybe an earthquake will come and pull it through the earth and pop it to the other side and throw it out into space." "I want a Porsche" could be responded with "Yes, I think a red one would look great in the driveway. Maybe we could even race it on week-ends!" Acknowledging the want as OK, is part of joining. Verbally imagining, imaging the blocks interfering with the want is eliminated. An adolescent says "Let's live in a big house on a lake," or if a child says that and adds "Let's have a merry-go-round on it." We might add "Yes, I'd like to have a roller-coaster circling the house, to ride any time I wanted." Offering the dream a symbolic solution, or a wish granted, a written title to the dream house, a toy red Porsche, or an imaginary role play granting the power to have the dreams come true can affirm and allow the enjoyment of the dream or wish.

Maintaining perspective and detachment

It's easy to get caught in another person's anger, excitements or disappointments to the extent of losing sight of the process and overall picture. Joining can be a very powerful way of encouraging communication, but if we over-join we might get caught in the same dilemmas or the same restricted options. It may be our place in the communication to see the larger view. In keeping a perspective we can be more objective; not indifferent, but a little detached. We're then able to provide choices, options and direction. Much of what is shared in crisis involves an expectation we join in the crisis reaction. To not panic can teach and clarify choices. We may share similar experiences or notice a similarity of this to other events in the person's life in a supportive way. This can help reduce the reaction and support a productive course. Our perspective may be different and needed, but even if rejected the message usually settles in for later review and may open up other options and angles at another time. Even if they don't share our perspective, if we keep a little distance or objectivity, we may be a better sounding board, less likely to get entangled in the issues. Emotionally connecting need not en-mesh us in the process. Often in communication, we become part of the problem, rather than the solution. When someone is very upset, sometimes we can use our body posture or do something physically to protect us from getting too far in or overwhelmed with the issues. Healthy communication is a balance of connecting and joining to the sharer and keeping a sense of our own reality and emotional well being while providing a perspective of caring detachment.

❖❖❖❖❖

Question, while keeping "Whys" to a minimum

Our questions can have several positive effects. Questioning models the quest. Critical thinking is what lies in the balance between criticizing and naive acceptance. To question, creates options and helps clarify. Gentle prodding questions enable the debriefing of hurts and shameful events of the past. Questioning opens us up to our motivations and can reflect lost insights and new possibilities. Balance is important, for over-questioning can create defensiveness and stifle sharing. A good interviewer will use a minimal number of questions with lots of room for open sharing and maintain a willingness to follow interesting tracts departing from the question. Life is a quest, for meaning, joy, connecting and understanding. To question keeps us on the quest, the ability to think lies in permission to question what we see or are told. Critical thinking and curiosity are the road to learning and both rely on questioning. It's a much greater gift to teach questioning than information. The questions may not give us information and direction, but they give us energy, motivation and the ability to find direction. Asking too many "whys" can lead to intellectualizing and alter the level of sharing from emotionally honest to intellectually reactive. "Whys" commonly set up a defensive posture and prevent open sharing. Some questions prevent communication. If we question the details or the honesty of the sharing it may be counter productive. In questioning someone who has been hurt, asking them if they are sure it happened, or if they are sure it was the way they described it or why didn't they tell anybody sooner can keep the person in a hurt posture. Sometimes the latter, "why couldn't you tell us sooner" may cause us to question our openness or their ability to trust us.

❖❖❖❖❖

Tell stories

Stories of our childhood told to our children, stories of us told to partners and friends, form a bond. When a partner is telling favorite stories we've heard before, a test of a loving relationship is our ability to stay and enjoy the telling. The art of story telling is an ancient and venerable one. For eons, history and craft have been preserved through the telling of stories. Meaning and spiritual values are imparted through the stories and myth. Examples and stories can teach and create empathy. The examples and stories told to mirror should reflect without duplicating exactly. The message we want to give is affirming the feeling of uniqueness without exaggerating it, to offer a sense of uniqueness without setting up isolation. Telling stories of the exact same situation, removes uniqueness. Telling similar stories may affirm the uniqueness while helping the person know others have been through something similar and have come out on the other side. We can show understanding in words, examples and stories. When we share a parallel life experience we create an understanding and empathy encouraging further sharing.

Stories shared of friends who have had similar experiences also reflects a clear message of the person has been heard and understood. A simple “I understand” will sometimes suffice, and using a story creates a deeper connection. Analogies and hypothetical situations can be used to do the same. If we share a story and it doesn’t resemble their experience, they’ll be able to let us know and misunderstandings can be prevented. Take care not to use the example or story to minimize the uniqueness of other’s experiences or to tell stories that overwhelm and diminish the listener’s experience. Within stories are opportunities to impart hope or alternative choices and perspectives. Many spiritual leaders have taught through parables and stories. The story comes from the outside but the meaning of the story still comes from within each of us and may inspire us to move forward.

Don’t promise what you can’t deliver

Often we need to make promises and commit-ments. As a responsible partner, spouse and parent, the willingness to commit to an activity or offer time is a part of our role. Promising what seems realistic and manageable will maintain our credibility and keep communication lines open. When we promise what we can’t provide, which we sometimes do to end a power struggle or avoid conflict, the inability to follow through may cause greater stress and struggles. A “no” offered before excess expectations have risen is easier to deal with than a broken commitment. We may have unforeseen circumstances making it impossible to deliver what we’ve already promised. In this case, apologies, compromise or compensation will undo some of the damage. Disappointments cause struggles but are a part of the process of living and must be grieved as a loss. If we genuinely do our best to keep our word, the people we are close to will know and eventually accept the times we can't deliver. Trust and integrity are established over the long run.

❖❖❖❖❖

Take risks

We grow emotionally, physically and spiritually through risk taking - especially the risk of re-jection. In communication we risk opening ourselves up and being vulnerable. In the telling of us, we risk our stories not being accepted. We risk feeling ashamed, ridicule, being ignored or our vulnerability being used against us. Those of us from shaming families have a more difficult time risking with present family and friends. We have more difficulty acknowledging mistakes and sharing at a feeling level. Rejections can cause us to fold back up into our shell. Rejection comes less from meanness or not caring, than from carelessness and not noticing or distraction and stress in the other person. Rejection by others reflects their struggles and forgetfulness, not our importance or worth. In family, we risk saying or sharing something inappropriate or making a mistake in what, how, where or when we do the sharing. We may be playful at a time when it irritates someone else, so we may pull away because our playful posture is childlike and children get their feelings hurt easily. Risk is necessary to maintain relationship and intimacy. If we can't handle rejection we need to go back and look at the shame and early rejections causing it. To enter someone's silence, someone's pain, someone's anger and ask if there is anything we can do to help, if there is anything they would like to share with us or if we can just be close to them while they do their processing is always a risk. The person may say "no" but just taking the risk gives a message of care and availability. Giving them the opportunity to turn it down doesn't change the offer or the importance of the concern within the offer.

❖❖❖❖❖

Acknowledge mistakes

If we've said something inappropriate or at the wrong time, in the wrong way, acknowledging the mistake can lead to an atmosphere of risk and permission to make mistakes. The acknowledgment of a mistake and an apology or amend may not immediately heal the wound or not salve the effect of the mistake, but it can heal the wound within us. Eventually, people who care about us will hear and notice our amend and rebuild the connection. Even more importantly, we are teaching openness and vulnerability, not just in acknowledging mistakes, but to do the risking. Risk always involves the possibility of mistakes. In a healthy open communication, the mistakes of others and ours can be processed without shame, ridicule or teasing. In some families, seeing a mistake is a chance to pounce on someone who becomes the recipient of pent up anger. To notice and affirm the risk is more important than rehashing the mistake. Most of us feel bad enough, we seldom need other people being hard on us for our errors. Focus on the courage to risk more than the error.

❖❖❖❖❖

Encourage forgivness

Discourage put-downs. In healthy communication gentle caring statements become internalized into positive self concept. Even firm assertive messages to put a stop to destructive behavior can be done in a posture of caring and forgiveness. Interrupt and discourage self put downs by re-framing the statement into a reflection of the feeling but not restating the put down. If someone is calling themselves names you might say "You seem to be pretty mad right now, do you want to talk about it?" We can let those around us know we won't listen to the words when they call themselves names, though we will listen to the feelings they have. We can affirm the feeling but not the put-down behavior. In active listening, it's helpful to repeat what's said, but not name calling. Forgiveness is not forgetting or ignoring, it's noticing the hurt or wrong and talking about our feelings and responses. In forgiveness we decide about future communication and seek amends. We may still have feelings about what we've done but the door remains open for continuous and respectful connection.

❖❖❖❖❖

Suggest alternatives to talking

Spoken words don't always come easily and may seem inadequate. The right words to describe what's happening within can be elusive. Relying solely on words to communicate, eliminates the possibility of communicating when words fail us. Try writing, drawing, role play or imagining. The time of deepest need is when it's the hardest to ask. Writing is an alternative way to ask. As we write, we clarify and decide how much of the writing we will share with others. It's an opportunity to edit or even toss away what we've written. Notes to ourselves of what to share can help us stay on track and remember what is important. Writing still relies on words, if we don't have the words, drawing is another alternative to communicating feelings or thoughts. Children's drawings are a powerful representation. They reveal themselves in their art. As adults, in our drawing our childness is revealed. Drawing can be a reflection of our history, conflicts, turmoil, noticing, wonder, need, attitude, depression or joy. Role playing involves playing out different parts of our dilemmas or conflicts as if it's in a stage play. Role playing helps clarify. Sometimes it can be done with words, and other times with postures or settings. We can play all the parts or we can have others fill in the parts and we direct. Role play is a very powerful therapeutic tool. Imagery helps us tap the inner potential of our imagination and creativity. Through our images we can communicate with ourselves and others. We can create analogies, metaphors, dream sequences and parallels enriching communication. Imagery can help us clarify dusty memories and open up further directions and choices. It's a powerful tool for insight and creating a healthy reality. Imagery is the communication with our soul through the mind's eye. The sharing of the image is the sharing of our essence.

❖❖❖❖❖

Keep expectations realistic

Especially the expectation for acknowledgment for what you are saying or doing. Anger and futility in our communications comes from our expectations of how things are supposed to proceed or end, or how what we say is supposed to be received. Children seem to have the job of not letting us know they have heard a word we've said. Even with partners and friends, the absence of immediate acknowledgment and response doesn't mean we weren't heard or the person won't respond. Kids hear and respond to everything, they just don't always do it on our time table, or in the manner we expect or desire. The fewer expectations or pre-planned responses and goals we start out with, the greater the likelihood of being able to follow and open the healthy flow of communication or conflict. When change does occur, it becomes easier to affirm and enjoy the result when we lower expectations and use communication as exploration for connecting and understanding. It's important to have expectations of those around us, matching realistically their journey and including freedom of choices. When our expectations become an agenda, or are unrealistic, they become reflected in our communication, limiting the freedom to share equally and increasing resistance. Take caution as expectations can be a set up for preaching and controlling.

❖❖❖❖❖

Talking is like checkers, take turns

Share equally, avoid being the perpetual listener or talking too much. True communication is missed by over or under talking. When we share a thought, and follow with a pause, we can let the other know it's their turn to respond to what we said or add something new. We may verbally request a response. Some of those close to us may have a difficult time with this, so actively questioning creates response or inviting new input helps them realize it's their turn and realize what they have to offer is important. Including children and their input in conversations teaches thinking and helps them verbalize thoughts while developing social skills. Accepting the child's input without condescension or over focus encourages healthy balance. Not allowing the child to dominate the conversation or interrupt too frequently can be done with gentle and occasional firm reminders. A children's time can be allotted where they receive the focus of attention just as some conversations will be for adults. When possible, a blend is refreshing and educational for children and adults. If we find ourselves regularly in the listener role with certain people, it may indicate they are less interested in us, than in themselves. They may expect us to be as interested in them as they are. Our listening gives some of the attention they crave, but usually not be enough. It may be an enabling posture. We enable their self focus to continue and we enable them to use us. Usually we'll drift away from these relationships rather than continue being used. Listening is a gift but can also be a role we get stuck in. Noticing this, being open and talking about it is a risk. Balance in the sharing and listening is a respectful posture and involves the risk of rejection. A good listener elicits much from others and also learns to share and tell stories. Sharing may be harder than listening for some of us, it might even be a more difficult skill to learn, but one is not more important than the other. *Balance of listening and sharing in conversation reflects balance in a relationship.* As a person goes through bad times, the need for someone to listen may dominate for a period of time, but over the long haul in healthy relationships, the listening and the sharing balance out.

❖❖❖❖❖

Guide and clarify rather than advise and lecture

We have within us, all we need to stay on a life journey of excitement, interest, intimacy and joy. Often we need guidance to facilitate the realization of our strengths. Advice, though occasionally fun to give or receive, usually teaches little and effects behavior even less. Remember that trying to change behavior with words, is like trying to drive a car with the horn. You can honk all day but never get out of the garage. It's how we live and what we model that teaches. Modeling openness, freedom and choices guides those close to us back to their inner resources. Through confidence, affirming and sharing appropriately, our families can be guided to their potential. Conversation reaches its highest results when it leads to enlightenment. This is the light shed on our binds, the opening of new options and directions, the clarification of values and choices. Over-lecturing can be a form of emotional and intellectual abuse. Our feedback becomes lecturing when we go on too long, when we are too forceful or intrusive or when our focus is to impose, rather than clarify and guide toward a resolution fitting the other's reality. We may lecture out of a need to control, show off or believe so much in what we're saying we get lost in it. But also lost, is the real connection and the communication. The only approach closing down communication faster than lecturing is blame.

❖❖❖❖❖

Reflect back binds, dilemmas and ambivalence

When those close to us share, the gift of sharing may be returned with a reflection back of the binds, dilemmas and ambivalence we notice. Binds are the no win situations producing feelings of hopelessness and anger. Binds occur when what ever decision and choice made seems to result in negative consequences. For example, "If I am friends with Judy, then Nancy won't talk to me, and if I ignore Judy, Judy will be hurt." Reflecting back the bind and noticing the feelings with each alternative still leaves choices. Affirming and noticing the bind and its results doesn't change the bind, but lessens the binding nature of the alternatives. A dilemma is like a bind with no apparent choice. In many cases it's helpful to teach that not choosing at this particular time is a choice and often a wise one. When we're ready, a direction will open up, including the option to not make a choice. Exploring the possibilities and feelings of different choices is another way to help guide the path. Ambivalence occurs when we see both sides and can't make our choice. The confusion in our heads reflects the ambivalence but often when the voices are shared aloud with another, they sound different and the confusion lessens. The sharing of our heart unveils the path. The very saying of the bind, dilemma or ambivalence may reveal the answer, and even when it doesn't, a door is opened and pressure and tension lessened.

❖❖❖❖❖

Support honesty

Be more affirming of the truth than confronting of the falsehoods. Supporting the honesty is more important than confronting the dishonesty or exposing discrepancies. Children and adults frequently speak in parallel realities. They may say something not real because what was real felt too overwhelming or scary. In the story still lies the truth of the feeling or helplessness. Supporting the feelings and true parts creates a safety for more truth. Shameful feelings may be the basis for the dishonesty. We do not want to enable dishonesty but over confrontation of the dishonesty brings one further into the encasement of shame stifling further discussion. At some point we need to direct the conversation toward the truth and share our feelings about deception. Putting ourselves in their position might explain the reliance on dishonesty. Intimacy rests on honesty and honesty comes with safety and trust. We need to build a gentle safe trusting relationship in order for the honesty to surface. The honesty of facts can often cover the honesty of feelings. The feeling level is where true communication occurs. Often, the dishonesty is of omission saying only part of the truth. How we respond to the part shared may determine the ability to fill out the story. Honesty is taught by modeling honesty. When we value and respond honestly and share with honesty, those around us learn honesty and an ability to express and celebrate the truth.

❖❖❖❖❖

Take it seriously without overreacting

We may take concerns and worries of the people around us, especially children, with a lightness or lack of seriousness minimizing or ignoring the true depth of the issue for them. The perception of an issue as serious makes it so. When someone close believes in the seriousness of a matter, it's serious. Our recognition and acceptance of this helps us present a more realistic perspective of the matter. Gentle teasing or funning of misery may on occasion help one through hard times. But even then, we can embrace the seriousness and the feelings and in our embracing the load becomes easier because it's shared. Puppy love, guests coming, lost toys, feeling too fat, homework or housework pressures may seem small, especially when we feel overwhelmed with our own life crises. The problems of others are as important to them as ours are to us. While seeing the problems of others as significant, don't get pulled too far in. We can overreact or participate in the panic. A little detachment and calm can provide solace as well as objectivity. We can maintain this calm without minimizing the problems. We can be the calm spot in the stormy lives of children, adolescence and others close to us.

❖❖❖❖❖❖

Teach process time

Don't rush in to solve problems or offer feedback. Wait a bit and give feedback when asked unless the asking is just too difficult. Trust the person to be able to work out the problem they worked into. Our confidence in them is very powerful and a supportive form of communication. Pause, and reflect how to offer what we have in a way leaving options open and encouraging the use of their inner resources. Model and support process time allowing the answers to appear - sometimes from within, and other times from without. The solution may come from the circumstances. Real crises are rare and can blow themselves out in a short time. Patience can be taught through modeling. It's easy to get caught in the need for immediate answers and solutions. Decisions and feedback offered in haste are often a waste. A little process time, a delay in answering may allow the integration of more experience, information and objectivity. We react frequently rather than act. Offering the space and time to step away from the immediacy of the issue helps healing even if the answer doesn't appear. Providing healthy distraction is positive action.

❖❖❖❖❖

Be pro-active rather than re-active

Pro-active means taking the initiative and guiding the course. When we see something serious coming down the line, it is time to get involved rather than waiting for the problem to develop. We can communicate openly about problems we see in the direction family members are taking or what we see developing with the family itself. If we're relocating, being pro-active means letting children know they might feel losses, experience mood swings, and could have a difficult time making the connection between the feelings and experiences, so there will be lots of support in doing so. We can give pro-active confidence in their ability to make the change, allow them the feelings and problems, and let them know it's a normal process. Being re-active is waiting for the problems to emerge and then trying to quell the following storms. Pro-active communication involves anticipation, the supplying of information, the providing of alternatives before the cross roads are reached. Teaching about puberty before a child reaches puberty helps one going through it. It doesn't do much good to have a conversation with a young married adult about dating when they are no longer dating. Sometimes neither pro-active nor re-active is the answer. The process may take care of itself. Most of life is process, and most processes and problems resolve themselves. It's OK to have problems and it's OK for old ones to go and new ones to come. Letting go of the stress, tension and struggle around the problem can be the best course.

❖❖❖❖❖

Linking and offering feedback

One of the most important gifts we can offer is link ing. Making the connections between the pieces. Experiences in life create feelings and reactions. Feelings set up certain postures, attitudes and behaviors. The behaviors and attitudes produce consequences. We often lose the link between each part. It's helpful in communication with others to have the link reflected back to us. Once we have the links, the pieces are easier to accept and change is easier to make. If someone's dog runs away and they feel sad, lonely and angry, they may not connect the sadness and anger to the missing pet. Once someone else helps with this awareness of the connection the person can accept the feeling as natural and do the grieving. If in their sadness and anger they snap at people and isolate from them, it's helpful if the link is made between this behavior and the feeling of loss. The link enables understanding and the possibility of changing the behavior. The impatience and withdrawing from others, causes people to feel rejected and begin to avoid. The link here is the one between the consequences of the impatient behavior and people avoiding us. One may not recognize their behavior is what set up the avoidance. If the behavior is altered and an apology is made, a relationship may be renewed or reaffirmed. But if one doesn't notice their own impatience or withdrawal, others will continue to isolate. The linking process seems to work best if we go backwards from the consequences which is often the presenting problem, back to the behavior, back to the feelings, back to a precipitating event or process that set up the feeling.

❖❖❖❖❖

Be genuine Self-disclose

Tell personal stories with honesty and openness. Sharing experiences can be teaching, clarifying and building intimacy. We let loved ones know they're not alone in their experience, others, including us have found their way through it. It's also a way of letting them know who we are. Keeping our sharing concise and interesting prevents overwhelming or boring people. If we're always in the 'telling' role, we learn little about others, and this may result in resentment of the people we're entertaining. Balance telling, listening to and eliciting the stories of others. Allow lulls in the conversation. Self disclosure needs an honest assessment of our role in the story and a willingness to accept feedback. Telling of our mistakes and vulnerability can make for better listening and offers a message of taking risks and making mistakes. Exaggerating a little, especially stories told primarily for entertainment value is OK and fun. Some teaching stories are parables and fables. Children love to hear stories about us, and even more the ones involving them.

❖❖❖❖❖

Don't take yourself too seriously

Often in our conversations we become defensive or over reactive to criticism and statements challenging our authority, perceptions or ideas. Our reactions may come from taking ourselves too seriously. The ability to change our mind, reevaluate ideas and accept the world thrives on differences gives us an openness and approachability. We need a perspective on the importance of our existence, and our connection with the several billion other persons on earth, as well as the place of our community among the millions of communities on our planet, and the place of our planet in the entire solar system, and then noticing the billions of galaxies in the universe. We are just a tiny part of the network of creation. We are important, but we do have a very, very small place. Even the seemingly serious events of our life will be soon forgotten, by us and others. Soon too, we will be laughing about some of our humiliations and smiling about some of our losses. Many of today's tragedies are tomorrow's humor. Minimizing our loses and problems is not the alternative. Respecting a process without escalation and over-dramatization helps us communicate. Having a sense of hope and humor about the future and the healing that comes with time gives us a great strength in our communication with others.

❖❖❖❖❖

Keep a sense of humor

A sense of humor can move us through difficult conversations and be the spark of healthy communication. The ability to laugh easily with others and ourselves helps others share with ease and enjoyment. Humor is permission giving. It relieves tension and anxiety, reduces the fear of mistakes and helps alleviate shame. A good sense of humor isn't the ability to tell jokes, but the ability to laugh at the anomalies, surprises and stories around us. Good humor and laughter binds relationships, it's the glue holding intimacy together. It is the cement of families and a reflection of a disposition looking to the eventual, positive resolution of our life process. We can be serious without being morbid. *Laughter attracts. Our laugh lines are life lines. Humor is what is truly human. Humor is the core of joyful communication.* Even misery needs occasional funning. Humor is a learned posture towards life instilling an approachable attitude and teaching patience and optimism.

❖❖❖❖❖

Respect privacy

We are often told the mark of a good relationship is the ability to tell all. We can easily push partners and children away with our need to prod and elicit more information. We all need to talk about what's going on in our life, but we need to do it in our time and in our way and we never have to share everything. Being pushed builds defensiveness and walls, forcing us further inward. Too many questions creates a reactive posture of resistance. *Secrets may keep us sick, but privacy is necessary for staying healthy.* Having to tell all is a violation of boundary. Our sense of privacy gives us the ability to share what's appropriate at the time. A respect for privacy is indicated when we share our part and let the person know we are available for what and when they wish to share with us. Allowing space and time also delivers a message of safety so the person may be freer to share at a deeper level when they're ready. People might believe 'telling all' is openness when it may be an absence of boundary. Respecting the privacy of mail, space, room, mind and heart, means we respect the person.

❖❖❖❖❖

Answer questions directly and honestly

When asked, a direct honest answer is the best response. Tough questions require time to formulate the answer. Rushing in with answers can produce less than desirable results. The space provides opportunity to check out facts and form an accurate and respectful answer. Answering questions is a way of giving from experience. It's an opportunity to teach and reflect in words what we try to model in our lives. Conversation partners are usually their most receptive when they ask a question. Clear, genuine answers given with willingness, open the way for more questioning. A posture of 'quest' towards life, the world, and education is the avenue for learning. Our patience and interest in the questions of those around us lead to the path of critical thinking as a posture towards learning. Our answers are never written in stone. We always get to make additions, or amendments. We have the right not to know. We also have the right to make guesses but it's important to let the questioner know that our answer is a guess or our best shot at this time. Our own quest should be filled with questions as part of the evaluation of effectiveness and genuineness of our culture and its activities.

❖❖❖❖❖

Build hope, cherish dreams while steering towards reality

When we over-focus on problems, presenting the road blocks, we may be damaging dreams and destroying hope. Guide towards what is realistic in a way respecting and enhancing dreams and hopes. Help partners and children see possibilities and move toward their realization rather than confront and destroy the search for the impossible. Gently guiding the dream without crushing it requires a respect for the dream of others even though it might not make sense or be meaningful to us. Our belief in them is reflected in how we treat their dreams. Our belief in them gives them a hold on their belief in themselves. Even if we don't believe in their dream, the belief in them might result in a surprise. People, with the right support, can achieve impossible dreams. Using what is realistic as a starting point and helping clarify a plan for its achievement may enable the going beyond what is realistic. Dreams and fantasy have a power and a fuel of their own. Offering what is real need not topple the fantasy.

❖❖❖❖❖

Mirror With Gentleness

Mirroring back what is said, without mimicking can give clarification and meaning. When there may be a misunderstanding, repeating what was said in another way can be revealing. To mirror gives us insight into the nature of communicating beyond words. Mirroring makes us approachable. Mirroring is to be in the style, language and attitude of the sharing person without losing connection to our own. Conversing in the style of the other without being a mimic, provides an environment where the sharing can continue. The best communicators speak in a style matched and blended with the listener. Speaking at their level is not talking down, but using words, terms, stories and concepts familiar and comfortable to them. Mirroring is communication equivalent to walking in their shoes. It is easier to build a bridge to a familiar shoreline.

❖❖❖❖❖

Touch

When communicating with loved ones, maintaining physical connection communicates the continuity and affirmation of the relationship. Holding hands when sharing stories, a touch on the shoulders, using intimate touch times as a time to talk, holding for fun or nurturing all maintain communication. When sharing disappointing news, a touch helps us hear and stay in reality. When reprimanding, especially younger children, a gentle physical connection lessens the shame response by letting the child know there is still a relationship, we have not gone away even though we may be angry or upset and we're not breaking off our caring of them. A physical greeting when meeting or initiating conversation sets a tone for more sharing. *Touch deprivation is the most common and serious form of abuse in our culture.* We often forget how much touch those around us need, especially our adolescents. They seem to not need touch, but in fact, they are at a time when they desperately need it. Appropriate touch can be playful, casual, light, affirming, affectionate, fun, rough and tumble, nurturing, pleasing, comforting and respectful. Whatever it is, keep doing it.

❖❖❖❖❖

Validate, investigate and encourage

To validate is to affirm. We offer validity to the experience and reality of others. Validation begins with assuming the importance and uniqueness of the other. It continues by hearing what they say as a reflection of who they are. Investigation involves getting and recalling the information applicable to the need or situation. We wouldn't walk into an important business conference or a tax audit unprepared. We need to walk into important communications with loved ones prepared. Information along with open inquiry are part of the preparation.

Understanding the stages of change in children and partners including developmental stages helps us communicate effectively. To encourage is to instill confidence, being the support and cheering section as well as the leaning and listening post. *Fear is the threshold of courage.* Affirming the fear and the willingness to walk together through the door of uncertainty we inspire the courage towards positive action and sharing.

❖❖❖❖❖

Avoid over-correcting or mimicking

When one is sharing they often share in the style, dialect and words of their age, gender and immediate culture. Sometimes in the sharing, a word is mispronounced, a sentence structure is incorrect, the wrong word may be used here and there. Our constant correction of grammar or words distracts from what is being shared and may prevent the possibility of continuing communication. Our over-correcting may be the result of perfectionism and causes stress, in us and in those around us. Sometimes perfectionism emerges from a personal sense of brokeness. Out of our feelings of being flawed we demand perfection and fear the exposure of our insecurities. When our children communicate in their flawed and childlike manner, we try to make them perfect so we can continue hiding our imperfections. Rather than correcting grammar, model varied vocabulary and use of appropriate sentence structure. Grammar is taught by grammar modeled. Grammar, sentence structure and pronunciation are not the essence of beautiful communication. *Congruence, naturalness, compassion and humor move communication beyond syntax and structure.*

❖❖❖❖❖

Approach with an intent to learn rather than to teach or punish

As parents, as caring people, we are teachers. The teacher must always be a student. 'The teacher who stops learning is a fool and teaches only foolishness.' As a student, if we go about our relationships with those around us with an intent to learn about them, about us, and what they're trying to share about their struggles, we will maintain and encourage open communication. The more we learn, the less likely we are to punish or shame. Even if we don't learn much, the intent to learn reflects our investment in keeping the lines of communication open. Damage occurs in families and relationships when the openness disappears. Denial fuels the forward movement of pathology. All families and all relationships have problems, but the only real dysfunction is denial because it precludes the possibility of dealing with the problem. Solving problems is less important than learning from the problem. If our intent is to learn about the situation and offer clarification, guidance, understanding, awareness and information the problem moves toward resolution rather than dysfunction.

❖❖❖❖❖

Communicate openly and frequently

We may believe we're saying more than we say. The conversation in our head is heard by us and no one else. Some of us are surprised when those around us don't know of our interests, feelings, plans or hopes, even though we haven't verbalized a word. Our expectations are so obvious to us yet without our verbal, direct statements, no one can even guess, much less fulfill or negotiate with these expectations. Give some time each day for direct communication, a sharing of feelings and thoughts as a way to let others know we love them by our actions, not our thoughts and thought-talk. Openness is not only saying what is true, it includes saying how we feel and sharing the parts of truth that may cause us embarrassment. Communication is the heart of family and relationship energy. The sounds of sharing reflect a family of caring and belonging. Openness teaches openness, truth teaches truth. The truth can be used to enlighten or punish, offer light or confusion. *A kind spirit ensures our communication will bring kindness.* Share equally, direct toward reality, notice, mirror, join, guide, enjoy, model, use third parties and outside resources.

Pathways To Intimacy

PART TWO

SURVIVING CONFLICT
Building Trust While Resolving Differences

Surviving Conflict - Building Trust While Resolving Differences

Introduction

"Resolving differences is the gateway to cherishing differences. The opposite of love is not hate, anger or fighting. The opposite of love is apathy. Apathy occurs when the conflict or resentment festers and kills the caring and noticing."

The history of humanity is an unfolding story of conflict. Conflicts have bred discovery, reorganized culture and have been Homo Sapiens survival of the fittest. The human posture is an attitude of readiness for conflict. Conflict with the environment, the elements, other species of life and above all with each other. Among animals, sometimes it seems as though we are a thin skinned, rather slow species with large brains!

Our survival has been dependent on our ability to anticipate, our creativity and imagination. The ability to imagine and anticipate danger producers fears and anxiety often giving rise to aggression. Our creativity allows us to build defensive and offensive tools and strategies theoretically quelling some of the anxiety and fear, but often elevating it. Our anxious/aggressive posture with the world is reenacted in the microcosms of our families and relationships. Our conflict within family stems from insecurity and fears fueled by our aggressive and defensive postures.

Conflict is a natural part of being together in a family or a relationship. How much energy we give to it is a reflection of the level of fear and anger we carry over from past hurts, losses and traumas. Interests, goals, choices or behaviors of one partner may conflict with the lifestyle of the other. People can have conflicting dreams, conflicting rules they operate by and conflicting values and priorities. The conflict must be noticed or it can fester into rage and hostility and eventually a numbness destroying the relationship or sense of family.

Differences

Relationships seem to develop in stages. One view of stage progression begins with being attracted to differences, we admire special traits in a person we are attracted to. Sylvia is very drawn to Peter's loose and spontaneous style while Peter admires the structure and neatness in her life. But with time, maybe Peter's spontaneity becomes sloppiness and seems out of control to Sylvia while to Peter her tidiness turns into picky, picky, picky! The very traits so attractive in the beginning become the source of their conflict and are difficult to forgive.

The next stage is to resolve the feelings about the differences, express the feelings, fight, let go or find a third party to vent to. Next comes the ability to tolerate the differences. Only then can Sylvia and Peter reach the more advanced phase of connection to come not only full circle but to spiral beyond. To not just be attracted to the differences again but to cherish the unique, quaint qualities of each other.

The critical stage in this progression is the sorting through feelings about differences without destroying each other or the relationship. Many of us never learned to deal reasonable with these feelings resulting in conflict. Differences especially those breeding anger can be frightening because of what we've witnessed in our families and culture. Many people have been hurt by anger and fighting. Many of us have lived with rage, aggression, violence, or the opposite extreme of cold, distant, punishing, passive withdrawal.

Sources of Conflict

Inner Conflict

Conflict experiences become internalized. Our inner conflict often stems from the double messages and double binds of childhood. Conflict with self also stems from the low self esteem resulting from past hurts, lack of affirmations and unresolved trauma. Further eroding self esteem and escalating our internal conflict is self blame, a survival mechanism for childhood hurts.

Inner conflict may also come from conflict witnessed in childhood, in our families or environment. Our parent's conflict with each other may become our conflict with ourselves and the world. This is reflected in our inability to feel safe and secure and causes the loss of our belief in the possibility of intimacy. Our conflict with parents may become our conflict with authority, higher power and a battle with our own vulnerability affecting our capacity for intimacy. Conflict with our siblings might be reenacted in our conflict with friends, partners and spouses creating blocks to intimacy.

The conflict with self is reflected through our inner dialogue. The voice within speaks critically, disdainfully with a level of self resentment. Negative self talk may be projected outward fueling our conflicts with others. The inner dialogue includes the repetitious negative 'taped' messages recorded during vulnerable periods of our life.

Cycles of Our Past

Many of our current conflicts are the result of past conflicts, traumas and losses. We may react to trauma by re-enacting it or re experiencing it in our lives until we're able to resolve it and let it go. Much anger, fighting and conflict is a recycling of older issues, many of us need to go backward to be able to move forward. In our family of origin, if we witnessed parental battering, anger or detachment we likely recycle the felt sense and sometimes the scenes of what we witnessed in our relationships with children and partners. The people around us may trigger responses belonging to events in the distant past but until we complete the healing process for the past we can't seem to alter the conflict of the present.

Shame Spirals

It is easy to get stuck in spirals of conflict. When a person has been put down and feels shame it can cause a hiding of self and a need to control and present a false image. When people crack our control or pry underneath the false self and enter our shame experience we may react with rage, anger, withdrawal or blame. When something goes wrong, our inability to acknowledge our mistakes is because our shame experience makes us feel as though we *are* the mistake. We become defensive and blame others for what goes wrong and the repetitive blame creates the shame experience in the other person. The continual blame and need for scapegoats maintains ongoing conflict.

Fear

An inexhaustible fuel for conflict is embedded fear. Our fear escalates when survival is threatened. We fear not having enough or there won't be enough to go around. Sometimes the fear is being exposed, the loss of face. We fear other losses - of power, control, property, loved ones, health, family, friends, job. Our reaction to fear can cause and escalate conflict. Some of us withdraw when scared, triggering fears of abandonment in others and creating conflict with no outlet because of the withdrawal. Many of us get more controlling, for in control we have the illusion of medicating our insecurity and anxiety. The control we attempt causes friction with others. We can even use anger and conflict as a way of avoiding the fear itself. Most angry, aggressive and conflict ridden people are deeply frightened but bury the fear with aggression.

Fear of abandonment is a basic and common fear producing most of our relationship conflicts. Those of us who were abandoned either physically or emotionally by either or both parents or other care givers, including siblings tend to reenact the unresolved abandonment issues in our relationship with partners and spouses. We set up the abandonment by choosing partners who can't handle intimacy or focus on difficult conflicts so one or both leave. The fear of abandonment can also cause a fear of intimacy. Being close means the possibility of being hurt, so we distance through conflict and are not so vulnerable. Another possible scenario based on abandonment fears is the joining of the 'cling on' race, holding on so tightly to our partners we cause a resistance in them, resulting in them feeling smothered or overwhelmed and fighting for freedom. Grieving the abandonment, placing the fear back to the original abandonment issues can relieve current pressure of the apparently unresolvable tension springing from fear.

Competition

Competitiveness can also breed conflict and generally stems from low self worth. To be able to compete is to be able to do the best I can. To be competitive is to beat someone so I can increase my self worth - to put someone down so I can be up, to feel on top only at the cost of someone feeling on the bottom.

Researchers have documented boys and men being more aggressive than girls and women and males being more competitive than females. This generality appears to be true in sports, careers and business. However, the generality overlooks a never ending competitiveness many women in North American society experience. The quiet yet constant comparison of their own body to other women, continually sizing themselves up and down to see how they measure up - seeking a winner and a loser. This silent warfare waged of body hate and physical comparisons is deadly for many women and a tremendous waste of life energy for others. Could it be men's competitiveness is simply straightforward and obvious while women's is more subtle? Is the one form of competitiveness a driving force for overt conflict while the covert competition forms a breeding ground for internal conflict and a downward spiral of low self worth? Unfortunately our internal conflicts eventually become our relationship conflicts.

Both men and women have enabled a violent society in conflict with itself. We live in a culture trapped in a fascination with combat and have an increased baseline tolerance for violence. We are fascinated with sports, war, business - we seem to practice and worship power. The power of winning versus understanding and acceptance of process and enjoyment of p1laying. If we take the posture of focusing on winning we may miss the benefits of reaching understanding. The process of conflict resolution is necessary regardless of our posture.

Self Conflict

Generally we're not very hard on friends. We cut good friends slack when they make mistakes. Yet, with spouses, primary partners and family members we can be very critical, pointing out every little mishap and error. The closer a person gets to us, the harder we tend to be on them. This is a reflection and projection of how hard we are on ourselves, our self conflict. If we are overly self critical and deprecating, it will usually ooze out onto the people nearest to us. When we enjoy self respect and self care it will likely flow outward to the people around us.

Many of us worry about having common interests and matching lifestyles with our partners. We yearn for wonderful and romantic passionate interludes. Sol Gorden, author of <u>When Love Is Not Enough</u> urges people to forget the focus on shared interests, great sex or dreamy romance. He describes the most significant aspect of any caring relationship as friendship. Put your life energy into being friends with you and your partner and the rest will follow.

Since the opposite of love is apathy, when there is still conflict, there is still energy feeding the relationship and there's still hope. Unresolved and repressed anger and resentment fester, becoming apathy and damage the chances for reconciliation. Apathy is the extreme of the conflict continuum. To heal the apathy it may be necessary to dip back into the anger or possible rage. Moving back through conflict we may again find friendship.

Conflict can pose as a distraction - keeping us from seeing and feeling deeper hurts, losses or financial woes. Conflict can absorb our life energy so we don't have to experience the feeling of emptiness in ourselves or in our families. conflict can be a way of maintaining distance, for if we get close to others we also become closer to their hurts and our own. We avoid pain, tension, conflict and yet create more in what we try to avoid.

Decreasing Stress

Much of what we learn and hear about maintaining relationships and resolving conflict is counterproductive. A common suggestion to increase excitement in a relationship is 'be spontaneous!' How can someone plan, work and focus on being spontaneous without destroying any hint of spontaneity existing? In the book The Dirty Half Dozen, William Naglers presents an almost 'tongue in cheek' list of rules for having a fulfilling relationship. The rules are generally the opposite of what many of us have read or heard before. The theme is to reduce stress and tension between partners. He suggests '*not* keeping the romance alive' since the pressure to do so likely diminishes any romance remaining. He recommends '*not* talking about *everything*' as we can drive each other away talking about every nuance and issue, it's better to focus on letting some things go. Our favorite rule of his, is 'don't fight fair'. We concur. It makes more sense to put our life energy into compromising and *not* fighting rather than to focus on doing it fairly. Besides, fair fighting seems to be an oxymoron. No fight is going to be fair because if life were fair there wouldn't be any fights.

Since fairness is not a constant and differences are, the conflicts in family and relationship are inevitable. In the interest of minimizing conflict and surviving it when it occurs we offer our suggestions for conflict resolution. We wish we had all the answers, we don't. These ideas have guided us through difficult times and many others report finding solace using them. In the spirit of balanced living and loving, we urge you to take a risk and try them out. Take what works, leave the rest. Above all else, trust and be true to yourself as you'll have so much more to give to others.

Finding Meaning

Conflict resolution is moving toward a flowing of the sense of process and oneness of creation. When we are dropped into unknown waters, the panic and struggle can cause the drowning. Reaching for inner resources of physical, emotional and spiritual strength, trusting the wisdom of past experience with knowledge of the waters, we can begin swimming with the current. Keeping faith and hope, we have the wisdom to know we can sustain ourselves until we find a safe harbor and caring hands. Just as we can stimulate the crises energizing conflict we can create harmony to calm it.

The following suggestions may be viewed as guidelines but are actually awareness to be called on singly or collectively. Some of the suggestions are further clarification's of the principles for healthy communication, with the focus here being on conflict resolution. Others pertain more directly to the issue of conflict. Their real purpose is to help us see conflict as a process, a journey through turmoil. We move through it, sometimes with grace and unscathed, other times, tattered and shaken by our own absence of dignity and self respect. Regardless, with faith we will move through it. We don't arrive at a destination, experience loss or victory but grow to a deeper understanding and acceptance.

On the other side of conflict lies forgiveness. To be self forgiving enables the gentle healing and acceptance of others. With forgiveness we don't give up the capacity for conflict. We are reinforced in our ability to fight for ourselves, what we value and what we believe in.

The process of conflict resolution is ultimately learning to accept and cherish differences, to give of ourselves without giving ourselves away. It's pursuing pathways of a tranquil journey and creating a peaceful posture towards self and others.

"remember real crisis are rare
solve the problems you can
let some problems resolve themselves
let some problems remain problems"
from Butterfly Kisses

Thirty-six Suggestions for Building Trust While Resolving Differences

❖❖❖❖❖

Choose your battles carefully

Not everything we disagree with needs to be fought out, not every issue discussed. Conflict causes stress and relationships are stressful enough. The goal is to reduce stress. Sometimes a better choice is letting go and a better process is to deal with disagreements with as little conflict as possible. Some issues not dealt with, will fester and cause damage. These require efforts at resolution. We can alter the issue, our viewpoint or our feelings. We can request change in others, the circumstances or we can change us. conflict resolution is merely the means we create the posture and circumstances acceptable to us. Many of us move from the extreme of not standing up for ourselves, a doormat posture to aggressive hypersensitivity over real or imagined slights. Balance and kindness are the best antidote for a life with conflict. When relationships are full of care, our conflicts will be careful and rare.

❖❖❖❖❖

Use process time

The best approach to anger, frustration or conflict may be a simple time out. It creates the opportunity to find a clearer perspective or new insights. Our anger can block our ability to reason facilitating a spiral into helplessness or temper. Taking a few steps back can interrupt the spiral. Distraction and distance from the situation may ease the tension.

Processing gives us time to regroup our feelings and thoughts. The old "count to ten" cliché can be helpful, but go for one hundred! Taking a walk, playing a game, reading, doing the dishes are all process time possibilities. Putting an argument on hold can be helpful, but it's important to not use process as avoidance or to call passive aggressiveness process time. Passive aggression is punishing by withdrawing, process time is gaining perspective. Sometimes the fight or anger cannot be resolved and the situation becomes a process of acceptance and coping. Time allows for this. Time enables us to be proactive rather than reactive.

Talk it out

Many of us tend to carry our anger within and be non verbal. Others of us get into shouting and fuming instead of talking. Verbalizing anger can prevent a build up which can set up acting out. Talking can help us redefine the anger. Sharing what is going on with another person may provide us with insight. ***Feelings we don't talk out, we act out.*** In talking it out, we feel less isolated and more connected, even if we do not feel less angry. Finding support, not for what we're saying but our need for saying it or the feeling behind what we're saying helps us move toward learning, action and change. Using the words of anger and having them heard helps diminish our fear of our anger.

Helplessness usually occurs when we are stuck between the fear and anger. Sharing helps keep the anger from becoming depression or apathy and loosens the grip of fear. Fear spoken is fear lessened. To risk talking out anger with another is an act of love and trust when done in a loving manner and safe setting.

Notice the anger to and around the person

We all need to be noticed but sometimes we hide our feelings and in so doing, we hide us. Notic-ing when some one is hiding or what they are hiding may cause tension and defensiveness. Noticing their response of defensiveness is the next step. This also lessens the chances for power struggles. We might hide our anger so even we can't find it. Someone noticing it helps us identify what it is. To hear someone mention our anger to someone else besides us, seems sideways and may escalate the anger and tension, but it also might give us a chance to hear about it objectively. We can then decide what to do without the pressure to respond, especially if the noticing is done in a non-judgmental way or does not involve a hidden agenda. A simple noticing can be done in a casual manner, "John seems angry this afternoon." Healthy parenting is noticing, labeling and affirming feelings and the same applies for communicating with anyone we are connected to. The noticing can include a clear message of the feeling being OK, even if the anger is toward us, "Susan is angry at me this afternoon." When we give permission in our noticing, the person we notice can move on. Most of us get stuck when we're not affirmed for where we are. Noticing also tends to diffuse defenses as well as the anger. When anger is used to keep people away, simply noticing we see what is happening can cause it to lose intensity.

❖❖❖❖❖

Validate the source of anger

Beyond noticing the anger it is helpful to acknowledge and clarify the source of anger in a supportive and non-judgmental way. The anger is less likely to become destructive and we're less likely to feel threatened or helpless in response to it. Defending the assumed source of the anger tends to escalate the problem and often sets up a power struggle with the person carrying the anger. If we are the source of the anger, becoming overly self-defensive may give more power to the anger.

Affirming the anger can diffuse much of it. We can validate without over analyzing or defending. Joining statements such as "That would make me angry" can validate. When the source or cause is ambiguous just validation and hearing the anger can be helpful. Excessive anger may be a symptom of another emotional or physical problem. Pressures, physical exhaustion, active addiction, fear, financial distress are just a few possible sources of anger to be noticed, validated and linked.

❖❖❖❖❖

Don't threaten

Especially with violence or abandonment. Some times in our anger we want to hurt or leave some one. It may be better to say "I'm so angry I can't talk about what I feel," rather than "I'm so angry I want to hurt you or leave you." There's a threat implied in spoken, violent urges. Threats of harm and leaving are too frightening and large for many of us to respond to. They bring up our shame and we spiral into more defensiveness and rage.

Never threaten physical harm and only threaten to leave if you have carefully considered it as an option for your health and happiness and are prepared to do it if necessary. If the threat comes up in a fight and you're not prepared or don't want to leave, simply apologize for threatening to leave and say you didn't mean it. We all say things in our anger we don't mean. The goal is to use fewer of those statements. If we hear the person say, "Well then leave or go ahead and hit me" it's important to see this response as a defensive reaction to our statement, not as the challenge or threat it may sound like.

Many of us have been abandoned and easily regress, feeling small and helpless when we are threatened. The abandonment may be a recurrent fear and theme in our conflict only to be dealt with by talking about and grieving the original abandonment. When we've been physically abused, we are at risk to abuse others, be abused or to threaten abuse. The debriefing and healing from childhood physical punishment must be done so it doesn't become a theme of aggressiveness and threats in our life and conflict resolution. ***A threat of violence is violence, a threat of abandonment is abandonment.***

❖❖❖❖❖

One thing at a time

People cannot fight about or defend several things simultaneously. When arguing too many issues resolution possibilities are lessened. The original issue we were angry about gets lost as the anger dips into and attaches to other imagined or real hurts and issues. An avalanche of upsets may bury the relationship and the conflict. As another issue comes up, note it for future reference, write it down or mention it for later, but put it on hold.

When many extraneous problems keep surfacing, maybe the real issue is not being addressed. Sometimes we fight about the symptoms of a core problem we're afraid to address and the conflict continues until we explore the primary issues. Being late may be the symptom of disrespect or irresponsibility, or passive-aggressive anger. Arguing about being late may cause us to miss the real issue.

Few people can truly focus on more than one thing at a time anyway. Too many issues create hopelessness and shame. One issue may feel manageable, "I can change one thing," or "Maybe we don't have to keep fighting about it," or "I can let go of my wanting you to change that one thing." As the list of issues grows, our ability to change or let go of it diminishes.

❖❖❖❖❖

Use sound when words don't work

We may not be able to articulate how angry we feel. Words can get in the way of holding on to the emotion. We can express it with sound alone, not using words, or not worrying about the words making sense. It helps finding a safe setting and a person to support us making whatever noise seems to match the anger until it feels complete or until the noise feels congruent with the anger. We may feel embarrassed but the embarrassment is a great trade off for the chance to loosen the grip of shame engendered from hiding our anger and rage.

The expression or sound can give rise to renewed energy and connection with our body. The blocked feelings create physical blocks and pain as well as tiredness. The physical expression itself can renew our energy flow.

We might need help with catharsis, a psychological term for getting the feelings out. People who stay with us will become less frightened of our anger. With a safe place and someone to hear the depth of the feelings, the person in conflict has less of a need to act out the feeling. If we can't express the anger as big as it is, the anger tends to continue, recycling itself in various aspects of our lives. Let anger be as big as it is, not as big as we want it to be or think it should be. Yelling or screaming may not be a tantrum or a threat, it might be what we need to do to be able to see and share how big the anger is. Using a pillow or beating on a mattress with a whiffle bat or tennis racquet can work wonders in relieving the tension and exploring deep anger. Encouraging a child to scribble as hard and long as they need to on large news print to show how angry they are, can lessen the grip of the anger and frustration. ***The goal is not to get rid of the anger, but to express it and have it, so it doesn't have us.***

It takes courage and caring to stay with someone when they express deep anger. Using a helping professional to facilitate catharsis is a gift we can offer others and ourselves, when the anger is more than we can handle alone. The expressed anger heals best when experienced and turned in the direction of its causes.

❖❖❖❖❖

Support assertiveness

To assert is to state clearly what we notice, believe or want. It's the balance between being withdrawn and being aggressive. We can be assertive in an emphatic way without backing down, although sometimes we have to compromise. To withdraw is to punish with leaving or silence and passive aggression. Active aggression is a threatening or violent posture used to intimidate people. When intimidated, people respond and comply, but only on the surface and may get even later in covert ways.

Aggression and withdrawal do not build relationships, they break down trust. Aggression usually sets up defensive postures in others causing responses of rage or no response at all. Swearing, threatening, throwing, hitting, and often yelling are aggressive postures keeping us from our goals. Our need for aggression is best left in settings where it's part of the activity or focused on inanimate objects or in harmless places. See catharsis above. It's not OK to hit ourselves, or use self to hit or collide with something else.

Learning assertiveness is part of identity development. Assertion recognizes and respects the roles and boundaries of those around us as well as our own. Our boundaries are a construct of our identity. The ability to assert what we need and want comes from knowing ourselves, not just knowing our needs and wants but recognizing strengths and capacities as well.

❖❖❖❖❖

Externalize rather than internalize

Feelings easily become internalized such as when we don't receive support for the appropriate and healthy expression of anger. Repressed anger becomes cynicism, hostility, rage, and even apathy and isolation. Internalized anger is stressful and can cause stress related illness. It sets up the sideways punishing and passive aggressive withdrawal. If we model externalizing with simple statements about our anger, the congruent connecting of anger in our voices, bodies, facial expressions, words and behavior is actually less threatening than withdrawal or resentment.

Externalizing means expressing, not getting rid of or getting it out of our bodies or giving it back to someone. Trying to get rid of anger sets up offending behaviors and failure. People who offend are persons who cannot handle their feelings and get rid of them at others or in ways causing others to feel badly. ***In healthy externalizing we have the feeling so it doesn't have us.*** Sometimes, however we need to hold a feeling in so we don't burden or take it out on people who are not involved. Learning to suppress feelings can help us make choices as to when, where and with whom we share them.

❖❖❖❖❖

Forgive and re conciliate

The primary purpose in fighting is to resolve feelings about differences. Creating an opportunity for reconciliation and a deeper connection is a step in learning to accept and cherish differences. Anger is a part of forgiveness. The beginning stages of forgiveness are first to recognize the wrongs done to us, second to recognize our feelings about the wrongs and thirdly sharing our feelings, sometimes with the person, sometimes not. Sharing depends on our safety and the nature of the wrong. These stages lead to the ability to decide on the kind of relationship we will have with the wrong-doer and a sense of acceptance and serenity about the wrong done and our relationship with the wrong-doer.

It is important for those around us, especially children to see conflict move through to forgiveness and reconciliation. Modeling is the only way we teach and if we model the fighting but expect the reconciliation to just occur over time, those around us may never sense, learn or believe in reconciliation. Time does not always do the healing. Leaving it just to time may set up a recycling of anger. Reconciliation is a part of the conflict process. Forgiveness is the core of the process.

❖❖❖❖❖

Steer to what it's really about

Sometimes we fight about the little things bothering us because the real or larger issues are too frightening. Many of us came from families with pathology and many problems. To survive we learned to ignore the big things but the little things drove us 'crazy.' We may ignore the violence and focus on small mistakes.

We can help others address the core problem by our noticing or verbalizing it and then giving the space needed. They may or may not continue the process but at least they have more tools if they decide to. It's helpful to have the anger redirected back to the core issue so one doesn't get lost in dead-end pathways or confused by wandering too far off the road. If the conflict is with us, the challenge is to help clarify the real problem without being overly defensive, affirming the anger while exploring the cause. It's easy to diffuse anger in many directions and never deal with the causes keeping the anger stimulated. Sometimes the cause isn't easily located so the anger hops around or floods everything. Our anger at our spouse or children seldom has much to do with them. On occasion we need some time to process and find acceptance of the feeling rather than figuring it all out. Sometimes our feelings cannot be figured out, but they can be embraced and shared.

❖❖❖❖❖

See both sides

There are many sides to most conflicts. While involved in a conflict we tend to only see one, ours or the presenters. As a friend or family member we can open our ears, eyes and hearts to support the perspective of our friends and family and affirm their feelings. Our goal is to be on their side without alienating or increasing the conflict nor distorting our view of the situation or preventing resolution. The conflict may be diffused by asking what the other side may be thinking and feeling, role playing both sides, taking each side and reflecting or speaking about it from their perspective, placing ourselves in their shoes symbolically. Presenting the overview and the other side doesn't have to negate the experiences of anyone involved. If the conflict is directed toward us, we can explain our position, or write about it as best we can in a gentle way. We will usually need time to sort it out because when in conflict, it's difficult to think clearly. In presenting our side it's helpful to credit and show understanding of the other position and acknowledge the possibility of error, misinterpretation and our own culpability where it exists.

❖❖❖❖❖

Respect the struggle

Don't minimize what others are going through, even when the issue seems trivial or short lived to us. It's difficult to see what's behind the strength of the struggle. We often don't know the previous events contributing to the severity of another's feelings. Old messages and roles about anger and fighting can escalate the problems in processing even a little anger or a small fight. Sometimes past responses to anger cause us to feel shame or fear about expressing anger.

When we acknowledge our anger it becomes very important to be around someone who will respond, not just to the anger, but to the resolution and forgiveness process as well as notice the courage and difficulty we face in being open and sharing it with others. Denial, shaming or minimizing can cause us to withdraw again. If sharing our feelings was assumed by others to be trivial we may feel like there is something wrong with how big it feels to us.

We then feel shameful of our struggle in taking the risk to share. We need to respect our own struggles and be gentle with ourselves in our expectations of sharing the 'right' way, at the 'right' time and following all the guidelines. None of us will or can do it perfectly.

❖❖❖❖❖

Use "I" statements

When sharing anger and perceptions in a conflict, it is easy to go on the attack and do a complete inventory or character analysis of the other person. This usually causes more defensiveness and escalates the conflict. Even when we're describing or confronting the activities of another, it's important to begin with I statements. Rather than saying "you make me mad, you're always leaving stuff around the house," it becomes easier to hear, and involves more ownership by us when we say, "I get angry when I see stuff all over the house. I would like you to be more respectful of my need to not live in clutter." The problem is ours, the feeling is ours, the ultimate responsibility for the solution is ours. The other person will hopefully hear us, and help with our problem which becomes easier when we own it rather than giving it away or blaming others. Inviting them to help with our issue is easier than telling them what is wrong with them. Recognizing our part of the problem maintains balance in the relationship.

❖❖❖❖❖❖

Use appropriate belt line

In a conflict, some of what is said is bound to be mean and hurtful. It is important to hear everything said and react appropriately. Sometimes we overreact and even mild confrontation can cause great pain.

It is difficult to resolve a conflict with someone who is hurt deeply by anything we say or any anger shared. The flip side is not allowing anything to hurt, not acknowledging the impact and refusing to react. Either extreme eliminates conflict resolution. The answer may lie in the symbolic concept of the appropriate belt line. When the belt line is too high, perhaps around our forehead, *everything* is below the belt and crushes us. We become the walking wounded. When the belt line is too low, near the ankles, we pretend detachment, causing isolation and bitterness. When our belt line is in the middle, some feedback will hurt, and we can respond or share the hurt. When there is too much below the belt, we can confront the unfairness or dirty fighting. Above belt feedback is more easily heard, understood and can be accepted. An appropriate belt line means we can hear and process in a fight, while still recognizing what is hurtful or unfair. It enables people to talk to us and our responses can be reasonable and emotional.

❖❖❖❖❖

Don't fight about details

We can get lost or mired down in details. The details of disagreements can overwhelm the real hurt or anger and prevent any progression toward closure or resolution. Details can also distract from the conflict and are so much easier to fight about or disagree on than the core issues. If one is late picking up a partner for an important commitment or celebration, and the anger surfaces later in the evening, the partner may say "I am angry because you were a half hour late." Our response may be "it was twenty five minutes." Eventually we begin fighting about whether it was twenty five or thirty minutes, rather than the hurt, disrespect or fear of the original source of the conflict. A more appropriate response may be, "I know I was late and I'm sorry." We may even affirm the real issue by saying, "It may have made you feel frightened because I could have been hurt, or discounted because I didn't think that you were worth being on time for. You are important to me and in a way it feels good to know you worry about me." We may explain why we were late or not, which is less important than affirming the other's feelings while not using details to defend or distract.

❖❖❖❖❖

Return to the real source of the anger

When we're angry, it's easy to release it with or at someone who has nothing to do with the anger. Usually this is someone close to us but may also be another group, driver on the highway, salesperson or ticket agent. When travel arrangements get messed up or there is delay, it is easy to be abusive or impatient with the ticket agent who has nothing to do with the flight departure time. If we have a difficult time at work or we're confronted by a supervisor earlier in the day, it's common to come home and yell at our spouse or children. Anyone who has a family can come home at any time and find something to be angry about and it isn't the real source of the anger. We stuff the real issue elsewhere and it can be triggered by the kid's manners or a messy room. These just draw the anger out. We need to review the context of our lives and the context of our day before projecting anger at those close to us.

For many of us, the anger is from childhood hurts. Angry, distant and controlling parenting from our childhood may keep getting recycled with our own children or partners. Sometimes the anger comes from childhood neglect which we recycle by not taking better care of ourselves, working too hard, or being hard on ourselves. The felt sense of our relationship with self floats out toward the people who are closest to us. Self anger eventually gets projected out as blame.

Our lives feel out of control when we try to control too much, especially in our families. The real fight may be a fight we never resolved with our parents or our siblings. It's too scary to be angry at certain people so we go for someone we are less afraid of. Anger at our children or partner may be displaced family of origin anger. If we are angry at one child more than the others, it could be we have selected a scapegoat for the anger in our lives, a recipient of our impatience and self-judging.

❖❖❖❖❖

Hang in there unless abused

Many of us don't like fighting or anger. "We hate anger. It always makes us mad!" We tend to withdraw either emotionally or physically when we're angry. Even though anger is scary, to be able to hang in there and share it or listen to another's anger is a gift we can offer. Anger can be dealt with, leaving can't. When we leave in anger, we leave the anger with our partners. They feel the anger of our leaving, the anger we left and the anger they started out with. They get a triple dose and may become rageful, which tends to justify our having left. They look crabby and rageful, we may look martyred and picked on, which further justifies our leaving, but in fact who is in control? Who is doing the greatest punishing? The passive angry partner or the active angry partner? It's devastating to another person to be ignored or left, both are very controlling and punishing behaviors.

Leaving when angry is a form of passive aggressiveness. We appear passive and withdrawn but are in an aggressive and punishing posture. Time outs are different than withdrawing. If the fight is intense, being across the room may feel more comfortable, but staying within eyesight and ear shot is part of healthy fighting. If there are threats, throwing of objects, physical hitting or pushing, leaving is the best option. If the fight is emotionally or intellectually abusive, leaving is appropriate.

Sometimes we feel abused even when we are involved in healthy conflict. This sense may come from false rules about anger or past hurts coming up during an argument or conflict. Sometimes only a third party, a referee, can tell us if the fighting style is abusive. We may be able to trust our instincts about this, but with fighting, our instincts may be over sensitized. On the other hand, we may not notice we are being abused because of our altered tolerance level for abuse from childhood or past relationships. Describing the words, setting and actions and getting feedback might help us decide if it was abuse or not. However getting too much advise from too many different places can result in confusion.

❖❖❖❖❖

Don't panic about the noise level

Conflict can be noisy. Congruence requires our voice matching the emotion. Being yelled at is not a good time, but we can survive it and possibly do a bit of noise making ourselves. What we yell can make a difference. Saying "I'm angry" in a loud voice, is not the same as saying "you're a S.O.B." in a loud voice. Yelling and screaming can release tension. Often yelling is used as a therapeutic tool, but it has its limitations. Repetitive yelling scenes may be efforts to control or dominate, and reflections of inner turmoil, rage or addictive and intense emotional acting out. Occasional yelling may be clearing the air.

Few of us like to be yelled at, and we personally tend to avoid evangelistic, emotional lectures and therapists who do a lot of yelling. Our reactions to yelling is greatly determined by our family of origin, especially our parent's relationship - particularly if it was angry and volatile, but also, one-sided or silent. Silent screams can be a great symbol for frustrating times. Anger catharsis is a small but important part of resolving angry conflict.

❖❖❖❖❖

Go blow for blow

Not physical blows, but take your turn. Say what you need to say and don't back down too often or too soon. Stand up for yourself. ***Talking is like checkers. Take turns.*** Fighting is like talking. Take your turn.

Defending yourself is a reflection of self worth and not needing or setting others up to do it for you - although it is wonderful if someone will help us. Adding what we notice and are angry about helps finding resolution based on equality, not sameness. It's easy to take the path of least resistance and allow the blow to go unanswered, but the peace ensuing is not a real partnership with self and other respect. It's too much like a dominant submissive relationship where we eventually relinquish the skill and the right to stand up for ourselves and notice our own anger.

❖❖❖❖❖

Don't take everything said seriously

Much of what is said in anger is not meant literally. It's an exaggeration or frustration and hurt put into words. A situation may be serious and reflect an intense feeling, but when the anger subsides the words or thoughts shared no longer apply. If we hear "I hate you," or "I never want to see you again in my life," we can respond with "I always knew you hated me" and three weeks later still believe we are hated when in fact the hate may have lasted two or three minutes. We may decide to go away or avoid the person for weeks even though they have apologized and insist they care and want to be with us ten minutes after the fight.

Feelings are attached to ideas or words. When these are shared in emotional outbursts they are part of the outburst not a permanent part of the relationship. Efforts should be made to not say things we don't mean, or know we won't mean later. When said, we can apologize. The harder job is to let go of the threats or hurts we receive and not punish back or hold them for later.

We all have ambivalent voices and desires. In the expression of our ambivalence or hidden thoughts and desires we may be freeing ourselves from the drives to act on them. If we can say "sometimes I feel like leaving" we may be more able to continue to talk about it and less likely to do it. Not processing the desire but repeatedly stating it, can also be a set up to act it out. The talk of leaving, to an excess may set up the leaving. Words are important. Balance is the answer. We need to be careful of what we say, but we also need to say what's going on. *Affirm and agree with what you can.* Use active listening skills without interrupting too often. Have a balance of interruptions. Diffuse scary confrontations by affirming the courage and the other's feelings behind the confrontation and agree with the aspects we believe valid. Affirming the viewpoint and the feelings lessens the struggle of the conflict.

❖❖❖❖❖

Seek areas of agreement

Fights are usually so focused on disagreements and searching for areas of disagreement we lose sight of how much agreement there may be. The fight may continue until there is a realization we both agree on the key issues.

It is imperative to say or show agreement where it exists. Some of this is done through clarifying our posture and asking for and listening to clarification from the other. Sometimes the areas of agreement are strong enough to allow some diversity of belief and disagreement. Sameness for the sake of sameness is certainly not a healthy goal or positive posture. Agreeing to disagree is another option. The goal of fighting is not to seek agreement, but to resolve feelings about the differences and to deal with feelings about hurts and boundary issues and values. Some values are worth fighting about and sometimes we need the other person to change in order to enjoy being with them. Change comes more from affirming and noticing where someone is, than in confrontation and fighting.

❖❖❖❖❖

Keep it current

No saving stamps or keeping score! When we don't deal with anger or resentment, we push it to the back burner, and carry it with us. It simmers in an old kettle for years until it boils over or a new problem turns the heat up and the entire mess spills out, we then overwhelm others with things they have either changed, forgotten or would like to have forgotten. It's difficult to deal with old stuff. We cannot change the past. It's challenging enough in the present. 'Saving stamps' means when we have collected enough and the other person has made enough mistakes, we can cash in our book of stamps for the right to punish, humiliate, or gloat in self righteousness.

We sometimes need to wait until the appropriate setting for expressing anger so anger won't always be current, but the effort to deal with things as they occur helps avoid the resentments or large conflagrations coming with letting it build up. If there's a history of a particular behavior being acted out in the present, it makes sense to support our data with the history. Constantly keeping score on the other person makes it difficult to have a spontaneous or trusting relationship. Feelings we have about older incidents are our responsibility to deal with in an ongoing way. New incidents however will bring up some of the old feelings even if we do keep current with expressing and sharing them.

❖❖❖❖❖

Show respect and care, don't rely on the other person to change

Demeaning and cutting statements may come easy when angry. Conflict and anger is not justification for being disrespectful. We can form our anger in a caring structure and not cut down the dignity of those we feel angry towards. We can respect their willingness to hear and their efforts to change, their intent and basis for actions as well as their anger and hurt while still being honest with our feelings. We can get angry with people because we care so much about them yet neglect to share the caring in conflicts with them. If a partner is angry because of careless driving, it may be out of fear of being hurt in an accident. Instead of sharing our concern, we may say "you're reckless, and you don't care about anybody or anything." It's very different if we say "I care about you so much I get scared and angry when either of us drives too aggressively." Respect includes not shaming or humiliating and letting them know the relationship is not broken and you will listen to the reasons and responses if they wish to share them. Respect and care for others begins with respect and care of ourselves. If we respect us and our anger, we will be able to share it respectfully and in caring ways. We will also be able to listen to the anger of others and hear the care and respect for us coming with their anger.

❖❖❖❖❖

Use appropriate settings and time

Some of the greatest fears and humiliations of child hood came from family conflict. When parents fight with each other or with children in front of friends or other people the results can be devastating. If the anger is deep and the problems serious, children can be excessively frightened during a parental conflict. They need to have conflict explained at a level appropriate to their development. They also need to know when there's a conflict and be able to notice the attempts at conflict resolution.

At times, and with certain types of conflict we need to find private space with the possibilities of interruption minimized. This may seem to take the spontaneity out of the feelings shared which in some cases, is desirable. Resolving conflicts before a large event, important meeting, special celebration, physical or mental examinations may be destructive. If the tension of the conflict will interfere with the event, resolving it before hand may be more desirable. If resolution of the conflict is likely to take longer, putting it off can be the better decision.

Going off together for an evening or a week end may be helpful, spending private time with the person with whom you are having a conflict. Working it out on neutral ground or even an unfamiliar place can facilitate and give us a different perspective. Finding a familiar place where both are comfortable is an alternative. Negotiating these issues can be the preliminary to resolving the conflict. The stage is set. Certain settings have significance in our lives. Using the setting to go beyond the conflict to a different level of values and sharing may help in the resolution. Going back to a place of close shared time may give one a sense of openness. If we fear spoiling the setting or memory with the conflict it may be better to go back after the conflict is resolved as a way of facilitating the reconnection. Appropriate settings with children need to be based in a neutral space where the child will feel safe enough to be honest and not so dependent on the adult. Bedrooms and kitchens are poor places and meals are poor times for conflict resolution.

❖❖❖❖❖

Write what you can't say

As in communications of any type we sometimes cannot articulate needs or verbalize our feelings in our relationships with partners or family members. It may be we get tongue-tied or don't feel safe enough to be vulnerable. We might also get lost in the defenses presented or feel too much shame about the anger or the need. We may be afraid of the responses or the need to defend ourselves depending on the response. Writing can be an alternative to sharing verbally. Writing leaves little question as to what is said. We can even do rough drafts before sharing it or express it in writing without ever having to deliver it. Some of us can be clearer with our words in writing than we can in speaking. There's also less chance we'll become defensive or deepen our own shame.

When we receive a written communication we may be less defensive and hear it better. We can go over it more than once and ask for clarification if we need to later without interrupting the flow of what we're reading.

Some guidelines for written communication may facilitate sharing: the writer maintains ownership of what is written. Even after delivering the communication, the writer can have the right to get it back, if requested before delivery. The writer has the choice of offering it to be read or simply reading it to the other. Sharing the writing by telephone can provide a sense of safety and distance, enabling us to speak more clearly. Writing can be also a practice for emotional disclosure.

Endearments and expressions of love are sometimes easier when written and may be more meaningful. Anger is difficult for most of us, but writing it out can prevent the escalation of temper and aggressiveness or defensiveness. In reviewing our writing, it's important to evaluate if some of it is our own rigidity, projection, or whether we are trying to dump or vent on others something not about them. The disadvantage lies in the absence of emotional connection and eye contact. These may be made easier after some writing is exchanged. Writing tends to eliminate the conflict about what was said or how it was said.

❖❖❖❖❖

Maintain boundaries - notice boundary violations

Boundaries are internal, a reflection of who we are. We maintain boundaries by maintaining and knowing our limits. *We cannot set our limits until we know our limits; we cannot know our limits until we know ourselves.* Boundaries are a construct of our identity. Our physical, emotional, intellectual, sexual and spiritual boundaries are interwoven. A boundary violation in any one of these areas will effect the others. Knowing our limits includes knowing what we can tolerate, the space we need, depending on the setting or persons, how much we can do, hear, work, how giving we can be, the amount we can deal with, internalize or receive, and how much data we can handle. Our boundaries and knowing our limits can also effect our eating, intensity, stress, work, sex lives and relationships.

Most conflicts are about boundary violations, the use of property, intrusiveness in our space or time, not recognizing ownership or responsibility, nor respecting limits. In the conflict we need to reassess our boundaries and be self protective without violating those of others. Being clear about the perceived issue and placing limits on the conflict itself is part of healing. We have the right to limit the range of discussion in a conflict as a part of boundary setting. Usually the difficulty in maintaining our boundaries has more to do with past violations than present conflicts. We need to do our best to deal with the particular incident on its own merits or perhaps demerits. Our children's conflict over boundaries are usually reflective of our own boundary problems. When we model healthy boundaries and limits our children will learn boundaries and limits. If we cannot take care of or stand up for ourselves, or if we do not respect the property, space and bodies of other family members, our children will act this out in regular boundary clashes with each other and us. Anger is a barometer of boundary.

❖❖❖❖❖

Stay with the anger

Our feelings are interwoven. When we react emotionally, it isn't with a single feeling but a web of different and often conflicting emotions. Many of us have a difficult time with our anger because it's welded to our sadness, it involves our shame and is wrought with fear. We may feel guilty about the anger and embarrassed when it's noticed. We may use other feelings to avoid the anger itself.

If we keep getting stuck and immobilized by anger it may be we're caught between the fear or shame and the anger. Associating the anger with violence can increase the fear. Just saying "this is very scary, but I'm going to stay with the anger" can help. We need to sort out the fear by acknowledging once we enter the anger, we won't be controlled by the fear. We can allow fear to give us wisdom as to how we express the anger, to be appropriate, judging what will be destructive and what will be helpful in meeting our goals and respecting ourselves and the other person.

Many of us cry when angry. It may be helpful to say the words, "I may be crying, but I'm really still angry." In our culture, many women have learned their tears are more acceptable than their anger, so when mad, they begin crying. Men have a tendency towards feeling more shame, more negative messages about the sadness, so men may actually use the anger to cover the pain. Our shame can be the vehicle to turn the anger inward and beat up on ourselves, refueling the shame. Anger can also diffuse the shame. This happens when we use our anger to stand up for ourselves, which is really a statement of "I am worth it, and I am angry about the messages saying I wasn't worth it."

Guilt also effects the anger, so it's helpful to embrace the reality of guilt and what we're feeling guilty about. Breaking family rules and being honest with conflict and feelings may make us feel guilty, but it can be a healthy guilt. Even being angry at the other emotional blocks to anger can help us enter and embrace. For example, being angry at the messages we received about our anger preventing us from being able to have our anger. Healthy anger is a reflection of a healthy person and a part of emotional balance.

❖❖❖❖❖❖

Rigorous, not perfect honesty

We need to speak freely and openly, sharing what we honestly perceive and believe, even be fore it's all perfectly sorted out. This helps prevent the anger from escalating. Those of us who have a great fear of making a mistake and constantly seek perfection have a difficult time with conflict because healthy resolution requires risk and willingness to make mistakes. Clarification can come in the process helping alter our perceptions and compromise. If we believe we see it all and have it down perfectly pat, we become more intractable and others will find it difficult to communicate, disagree, or resolve conflict with us.

Honesty has to do with honor. If the honesty destroys or tears down the other person or ourselves, there's no honor, ergo, not real honesty. The concept of honesty can be a club used to beat people. We can confront flaws, mistakes, or pauses in good judgment until the other person can't function at all. This can be done in the name of rigorous or perfect honesty.

The honesty with ourselves can also become too rigorous. The primary problem most of us have is being hard on ourselves. We are merciless with our flaws and mistakes and one might distort this by calling it self honesty. We need to use honesty as a part of our gentleness, offering the slack we give our better friends, to our partners, family members or ourselves. As people get very close to us, if we are hard on ourselves, we often project the hardness and perfectionism onto them. As long as we can keep a little distance we can tolerate and give more slack, but once we live with or form a primary bond with another person, the honesty we offer them is the kind of honesty we give ourselves. If we use self honesty to beat ourselves up we will tend to drive others away or hurt them with honesty. We honor someone when we expose the reality of us, our perceptions and our feelings. This can happen in conflict, in grieving, being vulnerable, being sexual, or just enjoying the world we see around us.

❖❖❖❖❖❖

Beware of triangulation

Speaking through or getting enmeshed with third parties is generally destructive and creates more conflict. Occasionally a simple noticing with a third person can be effective as a way of getting a message across but when possible, addressing the person directly with concerns is more respectful.

Triangulation happens when we bring someone into our relationship with another person or we intrude on someone else's relationship. Using a child as a surrogate partner triangulates the child between us and our adult partner. Mucking around in other people's relationship problems can be a form of triangulating with them. Let people deal with their own relationship issues, with our support. We need to resolve our own relationship problems rather than setting others up to take sides or take care of us. Sometimes we get between our partner's conflicts with children or other people in their life. We enter as helper, but usually end up feeling persecuted or unappreciated. It's disrespectful to assume people can't resolve their differences and need us to do so. When invited, it's important to respond especially when we see somebody getting hurt. We can offer comfort and ask if help is needed. If someone is being abused, we *must* enter. Noticing and sharing how we feel, then detaching as much as possible from the conflict process of others prevents triangulation. If other's conflicts seem to be hurting us or our relationships and tend to drag on and on, they become everyone's problem and must be dealt with as a family or community issue involving group or family process.

If we are closer to one or more of our children than we are to our adult relationships, this is usually triangulation and an inappropriate bond. There's a tendency when angry to complain to a third person and bring them into it, to not deal directly with the person with whom we are angry. We might even try to get information or alliances with this third person or child. Unfortunately this happens frequently in cases of divorce and marital discord.

❖❖❖❖❖

Repeat what we heard when there is a chance for misunderstanding

Again, repeat what we heard when there is a chance for misunderstanding. Do not repeat everything said. Again, do not repeat everything said. Repeat it verbatim, if it's unclear what is said and use different words if it is unclear what is meant. Words can be 'loaded' and may be heard differently than they were intended. Each of us may hear the same word and have a different reaction or a different meaning. For example, the word "separation" may mean a legal parting or a short time to focus or to process, or a period in our life when we have to find ourselves to maintain balance. It might mean abandonment, or just a little space, or it could mean emotional detachment, withdrawal or divorce. To hear what is intended, we need to check it out. Ask for the clarification. We might have an agenda or an assumption not close to the reality of what's shared. We may react emotionally to certain words not intended the way we heard them. Once we're in an emotionally charged state it's difficult to check it out, so as an automatic response in discussion or arguing, it's important to keep clarifying. Sometimes the word changes meaning with the inflection and so ask for clarity on what the inflection meant or if it was noticed or intended.

Non-verbal messages impact in conflict as much as verbal messages. Even though we don't repeat the non-verbal messages we can ask for clarification or notice them. The person may be unaware of the message they are sending. We can say "when you say that you care, but you're posture is directed away from me, towards the TV set while you're watching a football game, it doesn't feel to me like you're showing that you care." When we respond with congruence and clarity, and our own feelings to what is said and heard, it promotes clearer meaning.

❖❖❖❖❖

Don't blame, shame, project or judge

Balance flows from being empowered and responsible. Since anger is often a reaction to the acts of other people, it seems others must be responsible for our anger. It becomes their fault. People may be inappropriate and boundary violating and our anger at them is caused by their behavior, but we need to look at our control needs, expectations, self anger, old anger, periodic foul moods or nasty mood inflictions. We easily attach these feelings to something or someone outside of us. Blame can be an immediate reaction to things going wrong. Frequently we find our favorite target for blame - our partners, one of our children, our parents, God, even ourselves.

The need to blame often comes out of shame. We feel bad about us, so, if we make a mistake it seems as though we are a mistake. This feeling can cause a need to hide the shame so we blame others, otherwise we feel the broken self too easily. The shame-blame spiral projects the shame within us to those around us and sets them up to continue the system of shame and blame.

Projecting our shame and fear through our anger sets other people up to feel shame and fear, while increasing the feeling in us. To project is to see in someone else what is really in us. We see our kids as careless and irresponsible when, it might be our own carelessness mirrored back to us or imaged in front of us. Judging others often comes as a projection of how much we judge ourselves. If we're hard on ourselves, it's easy to be hard on others. Through our judging, we set up ongoing conflict. We sometimes judge our children or our partners based on unrealistic expectations or on comparisons to other people. We tend to find their faults rather than affirm and embrace their strengths.

Our anger may be a response to what others do. Sometimes other people do make us angry. Often our anger is a selected reaction or chosen response to the actions of others.

❖❖❖❖❖

Don't keep fighting the same fight

If the issue of conflict is repetitious and seems impossible to resolve, it may be a power struggle or the issue isn't really what the fight is about. Feelings of jealousy can be projected out as financial insecurity and control. Fighting about money may be a false issue to cover fear and jealousy. When a relationship becomes overly competitive, or the fight can't be resolved and there's been no compromising, even a little giving in feels like losing or giving the other person the power.

Outside help can give us a clearer perspective on the true nature of the conflict and help us move towards reconciliation or at least honesty and openness. It can also help us direct the conflict to the deeper issues. Outside resources may be from a professional counselor, sponsor, caring friend or spiritual advisor. It's important not to bring too many people into our conflicts because we may get conflicting advice, causing confusion and possible triangulation. Neutrality, gentleness and wisdom are the primary ingredients for a good counselor. Short term counseling can help in primary relationships, our relationships with children and ourselves. It's a risk to be honest about our conflicts in front of an outsider and for some of us it's an even greater risk to acknowledge we need help with resolving issues. The payoff is generally worth the risk.

Approach conflict with an intent to gain information without over-questioning

Whether the conflict involves us or not, if we see conflict in our family members, it is an opportunity to learn about us and them. Approaching conflict with an intent to gain information is not done necessarily to solve the conflict or problem. A solution oriented approach may put us on a dead end trail and may feel intrusive to others. The learning approach creates a path of support, listening, clarifying, affirming and empathy. In our learning, we can reflect back and mirror what we see and hear. We can try to help tap the inner resources of those around us. ***Within each of us lies our solutions. We know how to do us better than anyone else knows how to do us.*** Given guidance, safety and support, we will get there.

We learn through affirming and active listening rather than over questioning. Too many questions can bring excess pressure on a person and create more anxiety while moving the situation away from a feeling level. A few insightful and prodding questions from a gentle posture can help clarify. A barrage of intrusive questions may be stifling and lead to intellectualizing. We learn more from listening than advising or questioning. The question "why?" can move one immediately from feelings into analyzing or put a person on the defensive. This isn't always wrong, but the feelings may be ignored when they need to be affirmed. The "why" can come up later if it seems important. From our own reactions, feelings and thoughts we learn about us and the conflict. Looking within rather than without can give us growth and others the space to grow.

❖❖❖❖❖

Be flexible and willing to change and compromise

Flexibility can keep us from getting bent out of shape. *When we bend, we don't break.* If we're having too many conflicts with too many people, the possibility of needing to change is high. Our willingness to change isn't necessarily giving in or a losing posture in a fight, it's a posture of caring for ourselves and the other person. The changes mean we're moving toward our own potential and it might take conflict for movement. Sometimes a change is what we can accept in another, a control issue. It may involve a behavior reflecting disrespect to or for the other person. Placing yourself in their shoes and sensing what it would be like living with us, may help us view what we might change about us.

If we've tried to change but can't seem to, the problem may be deeper. It could be an addictive or compulsive process. It might be something based on deeper fear or unresolved inner conflict and we need to seek help. Possibly we need a support system for the kind of change we're trying to make - Emotions Anonymous, Adult Children Anonymous, Women's groups, Men's groups, a facilitated self esteem group or assertiveness training.

Our resistance to change may also be a defiant posture. Many of us have survived by defiance and rebelliousness, a posture of counter-dependence. Now our survival tool keeps us defensive, setting up power struggles with people who care and people in authority. It's difficult to change just because people want us to. It feels like giving up survival since defiance is how we survived. Do not make promises to change we cannot keep. When we promise what we cannot deliver we escalate the conflict.

Our change or willingness to look at change offers modeling, support, willingness and gives others permission to do likewise. It's much easier to compromise when the other side of the conflict seems willing to do the same. All of life involves change. There's no completely maintaining a status quo. When we don't go forward, we tend to go backward. ***Change involves loss and loss requires grieving. Part of conflict is the ability to grieve.*** Grieving includes the conflict within about accepting the changes in our life.

And thus, we end with the Serenity prayer. God, grant me the serenity to accept the things I cannot change, the courage to change the things I can, and the wisdom to know the difference.

Only the truly wise can love well,
fight well and let go well.

About the authors:

Marvel Harrison, a native of Canada, is a wilderness enthusiast and an avid runner, skier and canoeist who likes to play. She has a Ph.D. in Counseling Psychology, and is an author, therapist and lecturer specializing in a gentle approach to self acceptance. Marvel's spirit and zest for life are easily felt by audiences everywhere. She makes her home on a canyon in the mountains of northern New Mexico.

Terry Kellogg is a parent, athlete, counselor and teacher. For over twenty years he has been helping families with compulsive and addictive behaviors. Besides writing poetry, he is an insightful therapist and an advocate for vulnerable groups and our planet. Terry is an entertaining, challenging, inspiring, and much sought after speaker. Terry feels most at home in the Boundary Waters of Minnesota or on the pink sand beaches of Harbour Island, Bahamas.

Marvel and Terry, as program consultants to ANACAPA By The Sea Treatment Center in Port Hueneme, California design and facilitate intensive workshops. They are also directors of the *LifeWorks* and *Life Balance*™ programs at The Mulberry Center in Evansville, Indiana.

For information about workshops, other books, tapes, or greeting cards offered by Marvel or Terry please call **1-800-359-2728 or FAX 1-505-662-4044.**